ANOT

Focusing on the Power of the Cross

ANOTHER WAY

Focusing on the Power of the Cross

Barry Kissell

HODDER AND STOUGHTON

LONDON SYDNEY AUCKLAND TORONTO

All Bible quotations are taken from the New International Version, unless otherwise stated

British Library Cataloguing in Publication Data
Kissell, Barry
  Another way.
  1. Christian church. Symbols. Cross
  I. Title
  246′.558

  ISBN 0-340-50380-7

To the memory of Iain Roberts, my friend
and travelling companion for twelve years,
whose life and death epitomise the message
of this book.

ACKNOWLEDGMENTS

My special gratitude goes to my wife, Mary, for her encouragement and insights.

To Jona Skipper, whose own testimony is reflected in his cover design.

I wish to thank my secretary, Julie Evans, for another momentous typing effort.

CONTENTS

Author's Note

For thirty years I have sought to follow Christ. The journey has always been hard, and on many occasions I have failed miserably. However, despite the difficulties, there is no other way I would rather have lived. On reflection, it would seem to me that on this pilgrimage Jesus is always offering us an alternative, another way. This is invariably the way of the cross, which involves us in various degrees of suffering and rejection.

After leaving school I lodged in a boarding house with eight other men and an elderly woman. The woman was severely arthritic and bent over as she walked, supported by two sticks. In her conversation she was always bitter, critical, and argumentative. When I arrived nobody was talking with her, or had any intention of doing so. In this unresolved situation Jesus offered 'another way'. Practically, it meant forgiving her the hurt she was causing, and then seeking to resume and maintain a normal relationship. Such a response is costly in pride and patience, yet it is the way of the cross. Suffering and misunderstanding are involved – more so, if the situation is ongoing and never really resolved.

In conversations about God some people reason as follows: 'If there is a God, He must love and accept everyone, including me. I have lived a good, upright life, and believe that the good I have done is greater than the bad, and on this basis God is bound to accept me'. To this attitude of self-justification Jesus offers 'another way'. This involves finding God at the cross, where man has nothing to offer except his sin, and nothing to receive except God's undeserved love and forgiveness. The cost of this reconciliation is borne by Christ. Those who approach God this way learn to know Him and His ways.

Many times it has been my privilege to be involved with a family while a member is dying of an incurable disease. As the implication of their illness slowly dawns, dying people experience various stages of bereavement. Many feel as if they are being propelled into an abyss of hopelessness, separated from loved ones and robbed of life. However, in Jesus there is 'another way'. Through His own suffering on the cross He can empathise with the suffering of others, and because of His resurrection He can offer hope and eternal life in the midst of death and despair. Through receiving Jesus, I have seen such people be inwardly transformed, and die in peace.

In this book I have tried to show that in every aspect of the Christian life, the cross offers the disciple of Jesus 'another way'. It is my hope that you will capture with me something of what Jesus meant by saying: 'If anyone would come after me, he must deny himself and take up his cross daily and follow me' (Luke 9:23).

Chapter 1

A STRANGE REACTION

I once spent four weeks with a friend hitchhiking through Turkey. We entered the country from Syria and made our way around the southern coast, taking in the beautiful cities of Antalya and Izmir, before crossing the Bosporus to Istanbul and on to Greece.

At the start of the trip we were strolling through a small town, looking for somewhere to spend the night, when we had quite a frightening experience. I suddenly became aware that a man walking towards me was behaving rather strangely. His eyes seemed transfixed on to my chest. As we drew level he stopped in front of me and made a grab for my neck. I was wearing a gold cross which I had bought in Jerusalem. As he tried to take the cross he kept repeating the word 'evil', 'evil', 'evil'.

Fortunately I was able to extricate myself with the cross intact and we made our way through the back streets and out of the town.

During the weeks that followed I had a number of similar experiences as Turkish Muslims took exception to my cross. After a few such incidents my friend, who was not a 'committed Christian', suggested that I should not wear the cross again until we were in Greece. I reached a compromise and kept my shirt buttoned up when we were in crowded places. However, as a Christian of a few months' standing, I did wonder what all the fuss was about.

An Indian friend, Ashamme, told of a similar experience

Another Way

he had had in one of the Gulf states. He and his family lived in Kerala, the beautiful state in South West India. Like many of his contemporaries he had moved, without his family, to work in the Gulf during the oil boom. Whilst there his teenage daughter had suddenly died. Because of the climate, cremation is immediate, so that by the time he returned to his home, the funeral had taken place.

According to their custom, the deceased was photographed in an open coffin, wearing a wooden cross. On returning to the Gulf, Ashamme took this photograph of his daughter with him. During the outward flight he kept looking at it and, on landing, inadvertently placed it in his passport. At the Immigration Desk the photograph fell on to the table. The official examined it, threw it on the floor and destroyed it with the sole of his shoe. As he crushed it he exclaimed in Arabic that it was 'evil'. Ashamme was devastated but knew that he must not comment or he might be refused entry into the country.

Ashamme then proceeded to relate another instance involving the cross. In the Gulf state in which he worked, most of the contracts for major building and road works were given to foreign companies. Whilst he was there all the road signs were renewed. To signify an approaching intersection, a cross was painted on a black metal plate. This symbol caused such an outcry that the signs were taken down and painted over with the Arabic word indicating a road junction.

I was surprised to discover, whilst reading the *Qur'an*, that it explicitly denies the death by crucifixion of Jesus Christ. It states: 'They did not kill him, and they did not crucify him, but one was made to resemble him' (4:155ff). This teaching may account for the reactions of some Muslims to the symbol of the cross. However, I have noticed that such antagonism is much more widely based.

One Easter my wife, Mary, designed with others a number of banners to be hung in our church. One of these depicted Jesus on the cross. Its originality was in the view it portrayed. It was as if the viewer was standing behind and slightly above the cross, from where only the back of Jesus' head was visible. Embroidered along the bottom of the banner were the simple words 'Father, Forgive'. After the festival Mary was taking the banner home when she met a local person and they stopped to talk. During their conversation she asked Mary what it was that she was carrying. Mary explained how a group from the church had met and made a number of banners on the Easter theme. She then unrolled the one she was holding. The woman went an ashen white and, without commenting, hurriedly took her leave.

During the last fifteen years I have led hundreds of meetings in homes where the purpose has been to share the relevance of my faith in Jesus Christ with friends whom the host has invited. Usually such gatherings are conducted amiably and a wide range of subjects is discussed. However, when the subject of the cross is mentioned, strong feelings are often evoked. Certain explanations of Christ's death are acceptable. I have heard people suggest that Jesus' death was the result of a good man sticking to His principles. He was a martyr for a cause in the same way as Che Guevara. Others say that He was a victim of political and religious intrigue and suffered a miscarriage of justice as a result. Such explanations make for good discussions, but when the suggestion is made that His death somehow dealt with the problems of our sin, then the tone of the meeting can become quite aggressive or even hostile.

Whilst travelling in Sri Lanka, a Hindu girl recounted to me an experience she had had of the cross. It all started when she left her village to find lodgings in Colombo where she was training to be an accountant. There were many people staying in the house in which she lodged and, as a consequence, she could not find a place where she could be alone to study – in fact, the people who ran the boarding house turned the lights off an hour after sunset.

When walking out in the evening she had seen a light on regularly in a room attached to a church. She wondered if she might be allowed to study there, so she went to enquire.

She had never been to a church before, but she found the pastor working behind a desk in a room that turned out to be his study. She asked if it would be possible for her to use this room to study. He readily agreed and each night she used his desk to work on.

Whilst studying there her attention was regularly drawn to a figure of a man nailed to a cross. As she contemplated the figure she spontaneously wept. She found this emotional response perplexing and was determined to discover what it meant. Shortly afterwards a friend, who was a Christian, invited her to a meeting where I was speaking. My subject that evening had been 'The Death of Christ and its Significance'. She told me that as I spoke the symbol she found perplexing became clothed with meaning. Her understanding resulted in her receiving Jesus as her own Saviour and Lord. This symbol has a power to evoke many different responses.

I had been invited to speak at a series of meetings in Coventry, and during my stay in the city I visited the cathedral on a number of occasions. I would sit on a bench in the old ruins and watch people's reactions as they stood before the memorial to the original cathedral which was destroyed by German bombs during the last war. This is a simple, free-standing altar, above which is a cross made out of the charred remains of wooden beams from the ceiling. On the front of the altar are cut the words 'Father, forgive'.

As the Hindu girl in Sri Lanka was affected by the symbol of the cross in a pastor's study, so are many of those who stand and stare in this corner of the cathedral. Replicas of this particular cross have been made into pieces of jewellery which can be worn on a jacket or coat. I have noticed that all sorts of people purchase these. However, it is not just with people that the cross elicits strong reactions.

A minister once asked me if I would talk with a young man from his congregation who seemed to be disturbed in some way. When I first met John I found him to be outgoing and an easy conversationalist. However, as we talked I realised that there were a number of major unresolved areas in his

life. For a number of years he had been a homosexual partner
of a much older man. This man was wealthy and had a
powerful and dictatorial hold over him. John was basically
frightened and trapped in the relationship. Besides the
homosexuality, they were both deeply involved in occult
practices.

`Having heard John's side of the story, I told him that the
only person who could free him was Jesus. We talked about
this at some length, after which he indicated that he would
like me to pray with him. In the Anglican Church there is
an ancient service called 'The Litany'. During these prayers
we call on the power of the cross to defend and help us. As
I prayed for John, I asked that the power of the cross would
deliver him. I had hardly finished the prayer when John's
facial features changed to take on those of an animal. He fell
on to his hands and knees and made the most ghastly and
chilling sounds. Again I called upon the power of the cross
and he cringed like a dog threatened with a beating.

During my first year in the Anglican ministry I had to select
a subject and write an essay on it. I chose to write on the death
and resurrection of Christ and its meaning for us today. I duly
completed my thesis and sent a copy to the Chancellor of the
diocese, who was my tutor. After reading it he made an
appointment to see me. I well remember being ushered into
a large, book-lined study and invited to sit in an ancient
leather chair. After coffee he proceeded to comment on what
I had written. I soon realised that we were not on the same
wavelength.

New Zealand, where I was born, like western Europe, has
a church building in every town and village. Prominent on
all the buildings is a cross. It was a symbol I had grown up
with, but I had little idea of its meaning except that it was
the means by which Jesus Christ had been executed. Until
my early twenties I had never heard a meaningful explanation
of His death. However, this changed when I listened to an
evangelist preaching about the meaning of the cross. What
I heard him say introduced me to Christ. His message was

simple: he spoke of the cross as being the place where God
dealt with the problem of sin. It was here that Christ took
the punishment that was due to me. He died in my place,
so that I might be forgiven. After death, God raised Jesus
to life in order that we could, by faith, live in a relationship
with Him now. There are many theological interpretations
of the death of Christ, which I had analysed in my thesis, but
I had maintained that Christ's death for sin was its main
meaning. The Chancellor found this far too simplistic. It did
not take into account the views of other faiths – or those
people who had no faith at all. It made God out to be a tyrant
punishing His innocent Son for evil which others had
perpetrated. It was far too exclusive and would upset many
people.

For many years after this conversation, I was uncertain in
preaching about the events of the cross in this manner.
However, that was to change when I attended a conference
at Butlin's Holiday Camp in Morecambe. On the final day
of the conference Arthur Blessitt, the American evangelist,
visited and spoke in the canteen. He was fulfilling what he
believed to be the commission from Jesus to carry a life-size
cross on his back to every country in the world. Standing near
his cross, he spoke with great passion and fervour about the
death of Jesus in terms I had first come to understand at my
conversion to Christ. When he finished speaking, he invited
people to believe in the Lord Jesus Christ.

At the time I wondered what the point of such an Invitation
was. After all the two thousand delegates were surely all
committed Christians who had taken a week's holiday to
attend the conference. However, in my scepticism I had
overlooked the canteen staff. Suddenly, from all parts of the
hall waiters, waitresses, cooks and a variety of red-coated
young men and women made their way to where Arthur was
standing with his cross.

Within minutes he was praying with each one. Arthur still
continues his mission, carrying the cross all over the world.
I have myself encountered him doing this in India. Verbal

communication there is more difficult for a foreigner, owing to the numerous different languages spoken. Whilst Arthur has walked along the roads, carrying the cross, many people have been moved to tears by the inherent power of this symbol.

One Christmas I went to a gathering at a hospital where the Christian doctors and nurses met to celebrate the birth of Christ. After the traditional carols, the mince pies and the mulled wine, a speaker shared a few thoughts on the meaning of the festival. He graphically described the manger scene and made the poignant remark that, over the crib where Jesus lay, a cross was already casting its shadow. Jesus was born to die. According to His biographers, Jesus told His followers early in His ministry that His life would end on a cross. He did not view this as a disaster but rather as the climax of His life's work. It would fulfil all that had been prophesied about Him by the prophets of Israel.

In the preaching of the early Christians the event of the cross was the central feature. The Apostle Paul claimed that he founded a church in Corinth, one of the most notorious cities of the world, simply by explaining to his hearers the meaning of the cross. It was this experience which led him to claim that the message of the cross revealed both the wisdom and the power of God.

We are living in exceptional times. God is pouring out His Spirit. Rightly, we have been concerned to understand and learn how to minister the spiritual gifts which God is so freely bestowing upon us. It has been a special joy and privilege to enter into Spirit-filled worship and to see God's healing power. However, the continual blessing of the Holy Spirit will depend on how we understand and subsequently embrace the message of the cross.

Chapter 2

DISCOVERING THE WAY

On a trip to New Zealand recently I visited a sheep station situated on Banks Peninsula. This is a beautiful promontory of land with numerous inlets and a large, natural harbour which supplies the needs of Christchurch. Whilst staying on this farm I climbed Wild Cattle Hill. Reaching the summit I sat on a large rock and for an hour or more surveyed the exquisite grandeur of bush, rolling hills, and sea. On returning to the city I tried to capture in verse something of what I had seen and felt. I called the reflection 'On Leaving Pigeon Bay'.

Soft light of evening replaces the brightness of the day,
Shadows enfold the cliffs and re-wrap the gullies in
     their mysteries.
Parched brown hills crisscrossed by sheep tracks
Turn a pale yellow as they roll and cascade into the
     sea.

Leaving the homestead, trees line the track,
Covering it in deepening darkness.
A metal road passed a shearing shed and wound
     around the coast;
The sea splashed and gurgled in high tide.

Over the bridge and up the valley;
The mists hung low over the mountains.
Lights flickered in the isolated cottages;

Stars appeared around a crescent moon.
Joy filled my heart.

At the conclusion of that day I felt as if I had lived in a perfect world, that is, until I was brought abruptly back to reality by the late night news. Whilst I was in the hills a man had been knifed by a gang of youths in the city. A young girl had gone missing, having left home simply to buy milk at the corner shop. The television news editor had put together a medley of violence and carnage which briefly took us to Northern Ireland, the Lebanon, Afghanistan, Sri Lanka . . . even the weather man appeared glad to finish his report and leave, just in case the preceding twenty minutes had reflected on him in any way.

Such images always leave me with the uneasy feeling that something is drastically wrong, not only in the world, but also in me. Jesus pinpointed the cause. He said that the problem was deep within our personalities. As a spring bubbles up and forms a stream, giving life to all it comes in contact with, so out of our hearts comes the evil which, Jesus said, makes us unclean. For from within, out of men's hearts, come evil thoughts: sexual immorality, theft, murder, adultery, greed, malice, deceit, lewdness, envy, slander, arrogance and folly. All these evils come from inside and make a man unclean (Mark 7:20–3). The streams of evil from human hearts contaminate all with which they come in contact.

We live in a lane which, during a severe storm, was blocked by fallen trees. Most of these were cleared but a branch remained which became a source of annoyance to motorists. Early one morning I went to remove it with a saw. As I was working a van approached, and so I held back the branch to allow the driver to pass by. Unfortunately the branch was wet and slipped out of my hand, touching the window of the van. The driver stared at me with a face full of hate, and started to curse and swear as if I had greatly offended him. Although the van was not damaged and I had apologised, he was still shouting expletives as he roared off. He was reacting out of heart and, on reflection, so was I for although I did not speak, I felt a surge of anger rising up from within me.

According to Jesus we had both broken God's commandment to love our neighbours as ourselves. But did this matter? In all probability we would not meet each other again and, even if we did, the chance of the incident being referred to was quite remote. However, Jesus taught that the way we react to each other does matter. By such attitudes and actions we disobey God, and sin.

In our society the word sin has little or no meaning. The media usually prefix it to a description of some sordid sexual scandal. Unmarried couples co-habiting are often described as 'living in sin'. However, the word's main New Testament meaning is taken from the realm of archery. If, in the ancient world, a bowman aimed at a target and the arrow fell short, he was said to have 'sinned'. As the arrow fell short of its target, so we have failed to keep God's rules for our lives. We have not been able fully to love God with all our heart, mind and body, or our neighbours as ourselves. The whole human race has fallen short in this respect.

An equally vivid picture of the meaning of 'sin' is that of a farm gate bearing the sign 'Trespassers will be Prosecuted'. To sin also means to go where it has been forbidden. Sin is what we do against God and has many consequences, its main one being separation from God.

If I am having a conversation about religion I will often ask if the person believes in a personal God. To those who answer in the affirmative I enquire what their God is like. A number would argue that it is impossible to say as God is unknowable. I then suggest that the reason that we don't know God is because a barrier caused by sin separates us from Him.

The prophet Isaiah summarises the human condition in this way:

> Surely the arm of the Lord is
> not too short to save,

>   nor his ear too dull to hear.
> But your iniquities have separated
>   you from your God;
> your sins have hidden his face from you,
>   so that he will not hear. (Isaiah 59:1-2)

There is a popular assumption which is often expressed in this way: 'If there is a God, He must love and accept everyone. He must know that on occasions we all fail, as that is part of being human. Consequently He makes allowances'.

In sharp contrast, the biblical revelation of God is quite different. He is revealed as a holy God. This means that He is perfect and unable to be in the presence of evil without condemning and judging it. For many years I preached and believed this, but had little grasp of its real significance, until the following experience brought it into sharper focus.

I was walking through some woods in the grounds of a religious community where I regularly spend a day in prayer and preparation for my ministry. Turning a corner, I came across a grassy clearing. As I approached I had an awesome feeling that angels had gathered to worship God. My mind was suddenly filled with the ancient yet familiar words of the Liturgy where we pray: 'Therefore with angels and archangels, and with all the company of heaven, we proclaim your great and glorious name, for ever praising you and saying: Holy, holy, holy Lord, God of power and might, heaven and earth are full of your glory. Hosanna in the highest'.

Suddenly, in the Spirit, I saw a group of angels worshipping. It was beautiful. I stopped still and was immediately filled with praise and adoration. Such was the presence of God, I felt compelled to fall on my knees and prostrate myself before Him.

As I lay on the ground, my initial response of praise turned to one of awe. I was acutely aware of God's holiness and my sin. This resulted in much heart searching and confession. Subsequently many questions occupied my mind. I wondered how a sinful man could approach God, and if he did, what God's reaction would be. Whilst I pondered this incident and these questions, I realised that we are all accountable to God for our own failures and that, being just, God must judge us.

From this experience I felt I gained a little more understanding of the relevance of the Christian Good News that God and Jesus, acting together, had taken the initiative and addressed themselves to the problem of sin and its need to be dealt with in judgment. Consequently, they launched a rescue operation.

Whilst living in Cornwall I played rugby for Camborne. Every Boxing Day we had a 'derby' match against Redruth. It was on this occasion that I first met 'Bonso' Johns. Bonso, with his immense size and strength, played in the front row of the Redruth scrum as well as for Cornwall. He was the local coalman, and collected and bagged his coal at the jetty in the little sea port of Portreath. The jetty protrudes into the bay and helps shelter the small coastal steamers from the Atlantic storms. On a sign leading to the jetty is an instruction which forbids people from proceeding further when the tide is rising. One summer a visitor and his two sons, ignoring the warning, walked to the jetty's end to watch the thundering surf. Within minutes they were washed away. Bonso, who was working nearby, heard the cry for help raised by those in the vicinity and immediately took action. Diving into the swirling surf, he grabbed the father and brought him to the helpers on the beach. A second time he plunged into the swirling surf and pulled out a small boy. Although exhausted, he went in again. After disappearing for some time, he emerged with the youngest boy held securely under his arm.

God called His Son Jesus. This name means 'one who saves'. His mission was to 'save his people from their sins' (Matthew 1:21). From God's perspective man was under His judgment, destroying himself in a sea of disobedience from which he was unable to extract himself. God, in His love, sent Jesus who entered the surf to rescue men from their hopeless predicament. The place of rescue was the cross.

During His earthly life Jesus lived in perfect obedience to, and dependence upon, His Father. He never taught unless He first heard the message from His Father. He would not minister in power unless He first perceived that His Father had directly taken the initiative to heal the sick or demonised. Such was their absolute oneness that Jesus was able to say to the doubting disciples, 'Anyone who has seen me has seen the Father' (John 14:9).

Because of their perfect unity Jesus' cry from the cross of 'My God, my God, why have you forsaken me?' seems incomprehensible until we consider what Jesus was experiencing. It is apparent that at this moment of His greatest need He felt deserted by His Father. Scripture teaches that it is only sin that separates man from a holy and just God. However, this could not have been the sin of Jesus as He was the sinless Son of God. As Peter the fisherman wrote, 'He committed no sin, and no deceit was found in his mouth' (1 Peter 2:22). It was at that moment of apparent separation that the sin of every man and woman was placed upon Jesus. He became sin who knew no sin in order to lead us to God. Jesus received God's judgment on every evil thought and act perpetrated by man from the day of his first disobedience. At that moment, 'He himself bore our sins in his body on the tree' (1 Peter 2:24).

The cry of dereliction is followed by one of resounding victory. 'It is finished' He gasped before dying. During the three hours Jesus did everything needful to deal once and for all with the problem of sin. He died in our place, enabling us to be acquitted, freely pardoned and forgiven. This act of Jesus is the supreme revelation of God's love for all men.

Once, in my home town, a well-known farmer's wife became ill and died. Within a few weeks her husband was seen to be having a close relationship with her sister. This caused gossip in the tightly knit community. The rumours were such that the coroner ordered the body to be exhumed and another post mortem held. Scientific tests subsequently revealed that she had not died naturally, as was first supposed, but from arsenic poisoning.

Her husband went on trial for murder. This was heard before a judge in a little old colonial court room. I have always been fascinated by the workings of the law and spent a number of free hours listening to the arguments of both defence and prosecution. After work one Friday I stopped at the court room on my way home. Except for a few clerks and one or two sightseers, the court room was empty. I was told that the jury had retired. Within a few minutes the judge reappeared and it was announced that the jury were returning with their verdict.

When all those involved were seated the judge asked the foreman how they had found the accused. He replied that on a unanimous vote the accused had been found guilty. Suddenly the atmosphere was electric. The judge asked the farmer if he had anything to say before sentence was passed. In a panic stricken voice he said that there had been a terrible miscarriage of justice and that he was innocent. The judge listened intently before reinforcing the verdict of the jury and summoning a clerk.

Thirty of us sat in silence as we considered the enormity of what was to follow. The clerk was given a black cap and told to put it on the head of the accused. As he did this the judge said to the farmer that he had been found guilty and would be taken to a place of execution where he would be hanged by the neck until dead. Within weeks the sentence had been carried out.

The cross shows that God has put mankind on trial and found us guilty of breaking His laws of love. A sentence of death has been passed. However, Jesus voluntarily takes man's place and receives the sentence Himself. This death is followed by a mighty resurrection, making Jesus the Living Saviour of all who would come to God through Him.

When Jesus taught about His impending death He said that as He was lifted upon the cross to die He would, from the cross, draw man to Himself (John 12:32). This process started with a dying thief and has continued ever since.

Our team had accepted an invitation to lead a weekend for a Church of Wales congregation in Gorseinon. After lunch on the Saturday a young woman came into the hall where we were meeting. She was obviously a stranger and, having offered her a cup of coffee, I asked why she had come. It transpired that she had no idea that a conference was in progress but, earlier that morning, had heard singing and had come to investigate. She said that she wanted to find God. I told her that she was in a good place for such a discovery and invited her to stay and listen. I was involved with the next session and never thought of her again until I met her the following morning.

At the Sunday service I preached on the cross. At the end I invited people to come to the front of the church if they wanted to respond to the message. Our team was soon busy praying for people and I found myself confronted by the young lady I had met the afternoon before. 'What would you like me to pray for?' I asked. 'I want to know Jesus,' she responded. Wanting to discover something more about her I asked whether she was a regular worshipper at the church. 'No,' she replied, 'this is the first time I have been to church for twenty years'. By now my curiosity had risen. 'What made you come?' I asked. 'It all began last Monday morning,' she explained. 'On waking, my first thought was that I had to know God. We didn't have a Bible at home so I immediately went out and bought one in the town. This week I have been reading the Bible every day, trying to make sense of it. Could I ask you a question?' she asked. 'Go ahead,' I replied, longing to hear more of how the Holy Spirit had worked in her life. 'It's Jesus,' she replied. 'I like Him but find what He asks me to do impossible.' 'We all find that,' I said reassuringly. I then talked to her about our human nature which, in its behaviour, always falls short of what God requires. Next I explained that through Jesus' death on the cross we are forgiven and enabled, with Jesus' help, to live the life God intended. 'How could this happen to me?' she enquired eagerly. 'Close your eyes,' I said, 'and imagine that

at the foot of the cross there is a dustbin. Now go to the cross,
take the lid off the bin, and put into it those actions and
thoughts which you feel guilty about.' After about ten minutes
she said, 'I've done that.' 'What do you see now?' I asked,
sensing that the Holy Spirit was showing her something. 'It's
Jesus,' she exclaimed. 'He's standing with His arms extended
towards me.' Tears were running down her cheeks. As this
was happening she was kneeling with her arms folded. Slowly
her arms parted and she raised her palms. I watched transfixed
as she extended her arms as if to take hold of someone.
Suddenly her hands made a grabbing movement and she
stayed in that position for a long time, her face radiating the
presence of Christ.

Anyone who truly comes to the cross in whatever way must
turn from all he understands to be wrong. This can be
extremely costly. As with Levi in the Gospels, so with my
friend Tony. His coming to the cross meant that he had many
problems.

In the late sixties Tony had been a singer. He worked the
northern clubs, the luxury liners, and casinos in various parts
of the world. He was popular and successful, either working
alone or with more famous people. To avoid facing up to
responsibilities he used three or four different names and was
always on the move – that is, until he met Penny. They
started to live together, setting up home in a tiny flat above
a shop. Penny's mother was a Christian and invited Tony
and Penny to accompany her to a service at St Andrew's.
Within a few months Penny had come to know Christ and
Tony was made to consider the possibility of Jesus being alive
and 'knowable'. During this period I spent much time with
Tony as he struggled with the implications of coming to the
cross. There were two situations in particular that troubled
him. He had not paid any tax for fifteen years and he also
realised that, if he came to Christ, he would not be able to
go on living with a girl to whom he was not married.

One day Tony decided to act. By faith he came to Christ
and then rang up an accountant who, he discovered later, was

a committed Christian and able to give him valuable counsel. However, this did not stop the taxman asking for thousands of pounds in estimated back tax.

At the cross we face up to the consequences of how we have lived our lives, knowing that Jesus is with us and is able to help us put right whatever we may have previously done. During the subsequent eighteen months Tony and Penny felt as if they had lost everything. However, as the fog gradually lifted, they became aware of the blessing of the Lord as they started a new married life together, and encouraging business ventures opened up.

This realisation that we need to turn to the cross in repentance comes as we hear the Gospel message. Whilst on a tour, we talked with a young woman for whom this truth came as a bombshell. She had been invited to attend our meeting by a friend. It would appear that this friend was her only Christian contact. She said that she wanted to receive Jesus, but before she did she wanted to ask our advice concerning her present situation. A year previously she had given birth to a baby. When she became pregnant she was not married and was having regular sexual relations with two men, neither of whom knew of each other. When her pregnancy was confirmed, she told one of the men that he was the child's father. The matter was eventually taken to court and the man implicated was ordered to pay maintenance. However, she knew that this man was not the real father of her baby. She named him because financially he was in a better position to help than the real father. Now, confronted by the message of the cross, she was overwhelmed by guilt and wanted to be truthful about the past events. We could only pray with her, asking that Jesus would give her the strength to do what she had to do. Facing up to the consequences of sin is difficult but it is the only way fully to experience the love of Christ.

After repentance many people find God's forgiveness difficult to accept. This is because our culture insists that we must do something for everything we receive. We find it difficult to receive something we have not earned or paid for, and that is what forgiveness is. When a person has such a difficulty, I ask them to sit with their hands resting downwards on their knees. In that position I encourage them to confess their sins to the Lord. When they have done that, I suggest they reverse their hands and hold them towards the cross. Speaking words of forgiveness in Jesus' name, I place the gift into their open hands and tell them to take it into their hearts.

The year I was ordained into the Anglican Church I was befriended by an elderly Methodist minister. He had officially retired but was still active, preaching most Sundays and encouraging the younger ministers whenever possible. During tea one afternoon he shared with me what he had learned, from his experience, about leading people to Christ. Of the many points he made, one was to be particularly helpful to me. He said that when in prayer he brought people to the cross, he encouraged them to confess all the sins they were conscious of. Then, before pronouncing forgiveness, he made sure they confessed any incident that they did not think God could ever forgive. He noticed that it was often the 'one thing' which hindered a person from going in their relationship with Jesus.

The most vital part of any electrical appliance is the fuse. Across this tiny hair-like wire the power flows, enabling the appliance to function. Faith is the fuse which brings the power of the cross into a person's heart.

I had been asked to speak on the relevance of the cross to a small informal meeting in a private home. The host and his wife had invited their immediate neighbours and a number of work colleagues. It was a stimulating evening as half of the guests were not Christians and had little or no under-standing of Jesus and the meaning of His life. At about ten o'clock I formally closed the meeting, and talked with David and Pat over coffee. Pat had come to know Jesus six months previously, and was in the process of trying to help David understand what had happened to her. David was not antagonistic but, as an inventor in a computer company, he found it difficult to contemplate how it was possible to believe in something you could not see or prove. I took this opportunity to ask him how he knew that certain combinations of chips would make a computer perform a planned function. He replied that it was ultimately through experimentation. I then explained to him that becoming a Christian was also an 'experiment'. Again, I reiterated my basic theory that through His death Jesus Christ enables us to be forgiven and enter into a relationship with God. However, the only possible way to find out whether that was true or not was to apply faith. We had reached an impasse and I asked him if he would like to make the experiment. He said he would and so we left the lounge and went into the kitchen. I was not at all prepared for what was to follow.

I told David to close his eyes and in his own words pray that, if Jesus was present with us and able to forgive, He would make real that presence to him. I waited for a few moments, then invited the Holy Spirit to come and reveal Jesus. My prayer had hardly been spoken when David exclaimed that he could not see! Initially I thought he was joking but I soon found he was deadly serious. Not wanting to make him fearful, I told him confidently that what he was experiencing was quite biblical and I did not think it would last for long. Having made such a profound and completely surprised statement, I thought of St Paul who had a similar experience which lasted three days. However, I need not have worried because the Holy Spirit was resting powerfully upon David and he was discovering that the 'experiment' he was making at the cross was working. Within minutes his sight returned.

The work of Jesus upon the cross cannot be separated from that of the Holy Spirit. It is the Holy Spirit who gives a person the realisation that he is sinful and in need of God's mercy. As this truth dawns, He reveals Jesus and how He died in the place of the sinner, enabling him to receive God's gift of forgiveness. Jesus said to His disciples, 'All things have been committed to me by my Father. No-one knows the Son except the Father, and no-one knows the Father except the Son and those to whom the Son chooses to reveal him' (Matthew 11:27).

On a number of occasions a young man visited our home to talk with me about the relevance of Jesus to his life. We covered a wide range of topics, but I spent the majority of our meetings trying to describe simply the meaning of Jesus' death and resurrection. In between our talks I lent him popular books on the subject of becoming a Christian which we discussed together at our meetings. Unfortunately, I did not seem to be able to help him and we ceased to meet.

One summer this young man went on holiday to a Spanish resort. On returning home, he visited me; I have seldom seen a person so excited about having met with Jesus. I sat him down and, over coffee, asked him to tell me everything that had happened. Whilst on holiday he and his friends would sit by the beach in the evening and enjoy a few drinks. It was here that he met a group of Christians who nightly talked about Jesus with anyone who liked to join with them. Eagerly he recounted how one of the Christians shared with him something he 'had never heard before' (his words). The Holy Spirit had enabled him to hear. His new friend explained the meaning of the cross and how, through Jesus, his sins could be forgiven. They had prayed together and he had received the Spirit of Jesus.

During his sermon on the Day of Pentecost Peter focused on the death, resurrection and subsequent ascension of Jesus into heaven where He took His place as Lord and Christ. Many who listened asked what their response should be. Peter encouraged them to turn, believe in Jesus and receive the gifts of forgiveness and the Holy Spirit.

At the cross the guilt associated with our old lives is dealt with and a new power is given which enables a new life to be lived. This is the power of the Holy Spirit. He also makes real the nature of our new-found relationship with God. When preaching about the cross, I have often made myself a visual aid and stood with my arms outstretched. I seek to convey the truth that Jesus, with His right hand, grasps His Father's hand and extends His left hand to whoever would turn and take it. At the moment of response our sins are forgiven and Jesus draws His hands together, introducing us to and uniting us with His Father. However, for some people this is not as simple as it may seem, as I shall explain in the next chapter.

Chapter 3

ANOTHER FATHER

How often have I heard people say that they know Jesus as a friend, but have little or no concept of God as Father. One of the main reasons for this is their own lack of experience of fatherhood from their own father.

During the last thirty years we have witnessed an unprecedented breakdown in what was conventionally accepted as family life. The reasons are varied and many, ranging from the widespread acceptance of the 'new morality' which was advocated in the sixties to the cult of personal fulfilment, or selfishness, which has characterised the eighties. This means that, for many, their first consideration in any relationship is to do what best suits them. Such egocentric decisions are made in a moral climate which no longer has any definite boundaries.

When a marriage partnership finishes it is generally believed that the children will not suffer adversely. In fact if the parents' relationship has been particularly stormy, then the separation would come with a sense of relief rather than sorrow. Again, some argue that children are great adapters, and may well be better off in the long term with another parent.

Whilst at his primary school our middle son often stayed the night at a friend's home. His friend of ten always gave the appearance of being happy and joined in all the games and activities of the school with great commitment. However, his outward behaviour masked a sad and sorrowful little boy.

Our son discovered that at night his friend cried himself to sleep. The reason for his sadness was the break-up of his family and the departure of his father, whom he loved. During the next few years he was to live in a succession of homes with men he called by their first names.

Many fathers abdicate their God-given roles without actually leaving their families. When trying to help people with no experience of the Fatherhood of God I suggest that they open the door in their lives marked 'father', and describe what they see and feel. This can be a disturbing experience.

There are those for whom the open door yields nothing but a blank void. In their recollection their father seems never to have been present, and when he was they found it impossible to attract his attention or interest in anything that they found important. Father was distant and unapproachable.

For a number, like Peter, Father always demanded such high standards that all his life he felt an abysmal failure. He recollected how, as a teenager, he passed eight 'O' level examinations at 'A' grade and two at 'B'. When his father received the results his immediate reaction was to ask why Peter had failed to receive 'A' for all his subjects. Father could not be pleased.

When discussing fatherhood with Barbara she became angry, aggressive and full of guilt feelings. Her father had provided abundantly for all her needs both as a child and teenager. He was also generous with her husband and family but it was all at a distance. On reflection she could not remember ever having had a meaningful conversation with him about anything. Father just did not communicate.

For Penny, father was a person who betrayed her trust and could never again be trusted. She is now forty and her last memory of him is as a twelve-year-old. One winter's evening, without any prior notice, he left his family to live with a young woman. He disappeared from her life, never to return.

Richard physically cringed as he recalled the unhappy years he spent as a child. On occasions his father would suddenly

become irrationally angry. When this happened Richard
became the focus of his aggression. This often meant receiving
a severe beating for an apparent insignificant and minor
offence. For Richard, father was someone who was unjust
and, more than often, angry.

Judith wrote me a letter about her father. I had prayed with
her after a public meeting at our church. At the time she had
asked God to forgive her for the awful things she had done.
I had not thought it appropriate to delve further and suggested
that she quietly confess her sins to God before I pronounced
forgiveness in the name of Jesus. Her letter revealed
something quite sinister. When Judith was eight her father
had started to abuse her sexually and this had continued
regularly until the previous year when, on her sixteenth
birthday, she left home. Her subsequent guilt feelings were
because she held herself responsible for all that had happened.
For her, father was a person who forced her to do things that
she felt were dirty and unclean.

A friend asked me if I would talk with his daughter's fiancé.
Michael was a student in the final year of a university degree.
His problem, as he saw it, was that he was unable to get in
touch with his feelings. He never cried, felt compassion, or
even anger. Whatever his circumstances, he was emotionally
neutral. However, if anyone physically touched him he would
recoil and feel distinctively uncomfortable. As he talked about
his father the following picture emerged. He was an Oxbridge
graduate and successful senior civil servant whose emotions
were on ice. Michael was unable to recall any occasion when
his father had been affectionate to him. They had never
physically touched even to the extent of shaking hands.
Following the family tradition Michael went to a prep-school
where, in his final year, a rather strange headmaster beat him
three evenings a week as he studied prior to taking his
Common Entrance examination. The public school which
followed was, to Michael, an unqualified disaster. Michael's
father, and the father-figures responsible for his education,
were distantly cold and cruel.

Those who have such experiences of fatherhood have a major set of problems to contend with. Firstly, they are usually unable to know God as a father whose love and acceptance are unconditional. Secondly, in areas where they have been denied or abused there are suppressed, unresolved hurts which on occasions erupt in irrational anger, rage and criticism. Such experiences can lead a person to create a fantasy world in which they see themselves in circumstances which compensate for their perceived loss

Another sad aspect of this whole problem is seen in a man's difficulty in accepting the role of fatherhood in his own marriage. The model his father has given him is often the one he adopts with his children, thereby handing on relationships of potential destruction.

The journey to knowing God as the Father, with its attendant spiritual and emotional restoration, starts with Jesus. It involves seeking to understand His experience of Fatherhood which is the model for all those who come to the Father through Him. Following His affirming experience of Fatherhood at His baptism, He reveals the meaning of Fatherhood to His disciples through His life and teaching. However, it is not until His death on the cross, His resurrection and the outpouring of the Holy Spirit that the way is finally made for the disciples to know God as '*Abba*' – Daddy.

What I go on to share now is not just a theological reflection on the Fatherhood of God, nor is it wishful thinking, nor a set of intellectual facts which must be accepted by faith irrespective of any feelings. Rather it describes a journey of discovery that I set out on many years ago, which has given me a security and joy which I doubted was possible for a Christian who never knew his own father, had two foster ones and was adopted.

Our pilgrimage starts with the baptism of Jesus (Luke 3:21ff). Emerging from the Jordan Jesus kneels on the river bank in prayer. John, His cousin, describes how he saw a figure like a dove descend and remain upon Jesus. This manifestation was accompanied by the anointing power of the Holy Spirit as Jesus was later to say confidently, 'The Spirit of the Lord is upon me'. He had been affirmed in His Sonship by the coming of the Holy Spirit. The Father goes on to affirm Him verbally in three distinct ways.

Firstly, He says to Him, 'You are my son'. In this statement the Father is affirming the relationship which Jesus had with Him. It is as if He has put His arm around His shoulders and before men and angels proudly identifies with Him in their father/son relationship. My second son Timothy, whilst at school, played striker in the first XI. On one occasion I was watching him play in an important interschool match in which he scored the first two goals. From the touch line I exclaimed in a loud voice to all around me 'that's my son!' It is with the same sense of pride that the Father speaks at His Son's baptism.

Secondly, He affirms His love for Jesus. The phrase 'I love you' is the most intimate in any language. In this context it is without overtones of romantic love or friendship, but rather depicts an unalterable attitude of perfect acceptance.

Lastly, He affirms His delight in the way Jesus has lived His life. In the words 'I am well pleased with you' the Father underlines the complete rightness of the attitudes and thoughts which Jesus has had. It is no wonder that Jesus was unthreatened and secure in all His relationships and in the eventual direction of His life.

As the life of Jesus unfolds we notice that He is completely reliant upon His Father to find all aspects of His ministry. He tells the Jews, who at the time were trying to find the opportunity to kill Him, that, '. . . the Son can do nothing by himself, he can do only what he sees his Father doing, because whatever the Father does the Son also does. For the Father loves the Son and shows him all he does' (John 5:19–20). In the same way He is completely dependent upon teaching and preaching His Father's messages. Those who listened to Him preaching were incredulous at the content, knowing that He had not been educated in a conventional manner. To them He replied, 'My teaching is not my own. It comes from him who sent me' (John 7:16) i.e. my Father.

However, it is in the area of perfect obedience to the will and purposes of His Father that Jesus epitomised a son's responses to the Fatherhood of God. It is often propounded that Jesus fought the battle of the cross in the Garden of Gethsemane. It was here that He became vividly aware of what the sacrifice He was being called upon to make was going to entail in the way of suffering and death. Yet, at the height of His agony He was to submit humbly to His Father's will in this prayer: 'My Father, if it is not possible for this cup [i.e. suffering] to be taken away unless I drink it, may your will be done' (Matthew 26:42).

When Jesus introduced God to His followers it was as a heavenly Father. During their three years with Him the disciples had observed how He related to God through prayer and asked how they could discover a similar relationship. In response Jesus taught them what was to become the most well-known and used prayer in the world. In the opening words, He instructs them to address God in the same way as He did – as Father (Matthew 6:9).

This is a Father who, although unseen, hears every word spoken to Him and responds. The follower now no longer needs to be anxious about life's necessities because his heavenly Father knows of them and is committed to meet them. Most committed Christians would endorse this simple précis of the life and teaching of Jesus on the Fatherhood of God. However, the journey from here must proceed from His experience and teaching to Jesus Himself. It is only in Jesus that the true nature of the Father can be known. No one has ever seen God the Father, the creator of the world, as He is in heaven surrounded by glory and power. No one that is, except Jesus of whom John writes, 'No-one has ever seen God, but God the One and Only, who is at the Father's side, has made him known' (John 1:18). Jesus has always existed with the Father. For this reason He is able uniquely to make Him known.

John records a conversation which Jesus had with His disciples about heaven, which He called 'My Father's House' (John 14:2). He told them that He was going to return there and prepare a place for them. When He had completed this task He would return and take them to be with Him. Thomas was dumbfounded by such a statement, and enquired how they could possibly travel there. In His reply, Jesus made one of His most exclusive statements when He claimed, 'I am the way and the truth and the life. No-one comes to the Father except through me' (John 14:6). Anticipating their incredulity He continued, 'If you really knew me, you would know my Father as well. From now on, you do know him and have seen him' (John 14:7).

Philip echoed the thoughts of the majority when he asked Jesus to show them the Father – that would be all the proof they needed. Jesus answered him in this way, 'Don't you know me, Philip, even after I have been among you such a long time? Anyone who has seen me has seen the Father' (John 14:9). This is a mystery, the reality of which was only fully known by the disciples after Jesus had died on the cross, been raised, and from heaven poured out the Holy Spirit who filled their hearts.

During His death on the cross Jesus dealt with all that separates man from a holy heavenly Father. On the cross the God of creation was in Jesus reconciling the world to Himself. At the moment of receiving Jesus the way is made to know the Father.

It is at the cross that the Father speaks to us the words of acceptance and affirmation that He spoke to Jesus at His baptism. It is here that the believer becomes a son of God. He or she is adopted into the new family which the Father is in the process of creating. As Paul wrote, 'In love he predestined us to be adopted as his sons through Jesus Christ, in accordance with his pleasure and will' (Ephesians 1:5).

What this means came to me in a fresh way whilst on a trip to Sri Lanka. After ministering in a local church I was invited to the pastor's house for an evening meal. From his conversation I was conscious that he was particularly eager for me to meet his family. On arrival I was invited into a large room to be greeted by his wife. As we sat down he called his six children to join us and introduced them, starting with the eldest. The father glowed with pleasure as he presented his eldest son. I was surprised when the second son appeared as he was of West Indian origin and looked nothing like his brother. The rest of the family were of many nationalities ranging from Indian to Chinese. His love for each one was plainly obvious in the way he related to them. Over a meal he explained his family composition to me. He and his wife were only able to have one son. During their ministry babies were abandoned on their doorstep by mothers who were unable to cope. These they adopted to form one large and close-knit family. The father's pride, coupled with his joy and delight, reflected something of the heavenly Father's over His adopted children.

One Easter during our early morning prayer meeting for revival one of the group asked the question, 'Has anyone ever died for you?' Being early in the morning it took me by surprise. However, in the quiet that followed, I found myself meditating on his question. I thought of a number of parents I had read about who had pushed their child to safety only to be killed themselves. Again, there were those who, in time of disaster or war, stepped forward in such a way that they received the destructive force in order that a friend or even an unknown person might live. Eventually my thoughts came to the cross where God the Father gave the life of His only Son in order that I might live. What incredible love! From the cross the Father tells us that He loves us. The Apostle John put it this way. 'This is love: not that we loved God, but that he loved us and sent his Son as an atoning sacrifice for our sins' (1 John 4:10). As I stretch out to the Father at the cross, He tells me that He is pleased with me. The reason for this pleasure is that I have repented and believed in His Son Jesus. Jesus was once asked, 'What must we do to do the works God requires?' To which he replied, 'The work of

God is this: to believe in the one he has sent' (John 6:28–29).

We are now approaching the end of our journey but there is still a credibility gap between what Jesus has taught us and our experience. For some, their minds are still full of negative thoughts about fatherhood. Approaching the cross they still hear their own father putting them down; being angry; rejecting; withdrawing; abusing; abandoning; and his voice is over-riding that of our heavenly Father. Help, however, is at hand in the person of the Holy Spirit. He is able to make the Fatherhood of God a real experience for us. Paul writes, 'For you did not receive a spirit that makes you a slave again to fear, but you received the Spirit of sonship. And by him we cry, "*Abba*, Father". The Spirit himself testifies with our spirit that we are God's children' (Romans 8:15–16). This can happen in two ways.

For the majority of people this is a process. It involves calling upon the Holy Spirit as they work through the areas of hurt which they experienced when relating to their own fathers. This can be a painful period in a person's life because the hurt must be acknowledged and the suppressed emotions vocalised before the healing process can start. It is like lancing a boil which releases the infection, thus enabling cleansing and healing to take place. Once the hurtful emotions are released and the healing process starts then the Holy Spirit makes new the thought patterns. Instead of recoiling in fear or anger, the mind receives signals of love and acceptance as the believer worships his heavenly Father. By cleansing away the negative and destructive, the Holy Spirit enables the human spirit to respond to His presence with cries of '*Abba*, Father'.

However, there are occasions when the Holy Spirit by-passes the process I have described, and heals and restores a person within a relatively short period. On a ministry trip to Wales we conducted a series of one-night meetings. After one such a meeting a young wife and mother asked for prayer. Because of a bereavement as a young child she had, in her own words, 'no experience of fatherhood' and although she

trusted in Jesus, God the Father was unknown. As we prayed
I asked the Holy Spirit to come and reveal the Fatherhood
of God to her. What followed was both wonderful and awe-
inspiring. After about thirty minutes she started to cry out,
'No more, Lord, please no more, I cannot take any more.'
With that she slid to the ground and lay there for a long time,
her face radiating peace and a beautiful smile.

Later that evening she recalled what had happened.
Following the prayer she felt waves of love gently flowing over
her. These gradually increased in intensity until she felt as
if she was unable to receive any more. It was at that moment
she seemed to fall into loving arms. Maybe Paul had such
an experience in mind when he wrote, 'God has poured out
his love into our hearts by the Holy Spirit, whom he has given
us' (Romans 5:5). This young woman subsequently had no
doubts that God was her loving heavenly Father.

In the joy of meeting the Father there is the danger of
overlooking the incredible cost to God that such a meeting
involves. Firstly, He had to send His only begotten Son, whom
He loved, into the world and watch as we rejected, abused
and crucified Him. On the other hand, Jesus voluntarily
responded to His Father's request and allowed Himself, for
our sake, to be born as a man and to assume the position of
a slave. He humbled Himself even further by dying in our
place on the cross. It was His sacrificial death that removed
the barrier of sin which separated us from the Father. It is
solely through His death that friendship with the Father
becomes a reality for all who receive Jesus.

Chapter 4

'DADDY, I LOVE YOU VERY MUCH'

On the 8th November 1987 our team was staying with Cecil and Myrtle Kerr and the Christian community which they founded in Rostrevor, a seaside town a few miles from the border town of Newry. During the afternoon the radio was broadcasting news about the bomb explosion at the Remembrance Day service in Enniskillen. As names of casualties were released, it was discovered that one of the victims had been a regular visitor to the community's Summer Bible Camp. Ten others had been killed with him and sixty-three injured in the explosion. The following morning I heard Gordon Wilson, a survivor, being interviewed on radio and subsequently on television. Gordon had taken his twenty-year-old daughter Marie with him to the Cenotaph for the Remembrance Service. Marie, a student nurse at the Belfast Royal Victoria Hospital, was home on a few days' leave. He told how they had stood together waiting for the parade to arrive when suddenly there was an enormous explosion. As the dust subsided he found himself under six feet of rubble. Except for pain in his right shoulder, he was not hurt and immediately shouted to Marie, asking her if she was all right. She answered in the affirmative and managed to find and hold his hand. Whilst they lay side by side, waiting to be rescued, he asked a further four times whether she was all right and on each occasion she replied she was. When he asked her the fifth time, 'Are you all right, Marie?' she said, 'Daddy, I love you very much.' These were her last words she spoke to him, as she lost consciousness. She was rushed to Erne Hospital where, with her mother at her side, she died.

The interviewer asked Gordon Wilson what his attitude was towards those who had perpetrated such an atrocity. With deep emotion he said simply, 'I bear no ill. Talk of retaliation is not going to bring her back to life. She was a great wee lassie. She loved her profession. She was a pet and she died. I prayed for those responsible last night. She's in heaven and we'll meet again. Don't ask me, please, for a purpose. I don't have an answer, but I know that there has to be a plan. If I did not think that, I would commit suicide. It is part of a wider plan and God is good and we shall meet again.'

Gordon's words of forgiveness spoke into the darkness with more power than many years of political and religious rhetoric. His immense darkness was caused by the sorrow of losing a much-loved daughter in tragic circumstances brought about by the violence in other men's hearts. Rising up out of the darkness was the power of Christ within him, pronouncing forgiveness.

One of the great joys of living in Britain is to be able to experience the four seasons year by year. We live in Chorleywood, a village which takes its name from the predominance of trees in the area. From our home we watch as the buds of spring become the light green of early summer. We enjoy hearing the buzz of insects before the leaves change colour and autumnal storms denude the deciduous trees, heralding the start of winter. In northern Europe the whole of creation is caught up in this continuous cycle of change and decay and new life.

Man is also locked into cycles from which he is unable to free himself. Marie Wilson was an innocent victim of those caught in the cycle of violence. Within the community, one group was violent to another. They responded likewise and locked themselves into an unending cycle of retaliation and revenge in which neither mercy nor forgiveness were ever shown.

Violence is not confined to actions. It also involves spoken

words. I was staying at a vicarage in the North of England
and was asked if I would talk with a couple who were having
marriage difficulties. As I greeted them at the door I could
feel the antagonism and bitterness. Before we talked I
suggested it was important that we listen to each other and
not interrupt, even if we strongly disagreed with what was
being said. Firstly the wife described her grievances. She
accused her husband of never listening and living a purely
selfish life. When it was his turn, he spoke of her coldness
and lack of affection. When they came to respond to each
other's accusations they spoke the hardest words and could
hardly wait to criticise and blame. For three years they had
been locked in a vicious cycle by their spoken words.

Within the context of His death, Jesus experienced cold,
calculated violence against Himself. Because of his fear of men
Pilate, before whom Jesus was tried, washed his hands of the
whole affair. Once a year it was a tradition that the governor
release from prison any criminal chosen by the crowd. Having
pronounced Jesus innocent, he offered to release Him.
However, encouraged by Jesus' enemies, the crowd asked for
a notorious prisoner named Barabbas instead.

After this blatant miscarriage of justice Jesus was flogged,
brutalised and finally hung on a cross to die in intense pain.
During all the events of that terrible day, Jesus neither did
nor said anything to those who were attacking Him. In
contrast, He spoke words of forgiveness to those responsible.
By His reaction He was saying that violence was going to stop
at His cross. In His death He broke its power and thereby
established a place where men could find peace through
forgiveness.

Gordon Wilson illustrates this power, as does the father of
a little Maori girl whose story I came across during a recent
tour in New Zealand. In 1835 a party of Maoris, travelling
through the bush in the interior of the North Island, camped
one night near the Wairere Falls on the Waihou river. Some
hostile natives saw their camp fire, crept down and murdered
a little girl named Tarore. She had placed under her head

a copy of the Gospel of Mark in Maori which she had been taught to read at one of the mission stations. With a heavy heart her father, Ngakuku, a Christian chief, carried her body to the mission station. Though weighed down with grief he told the missionary he had resolved, after thinking it out, not to cause more bloodshed by carrying on the feud; that he would not take *utu* (revenge) for the terrible wrong he had suffered. This one act of forgiveness led to a powerful moving of the Holy Spirit amongst the tribes.

Forgiveness is always costly – it cost Jesus His life. Once we have entered into this forgiven relationship with Jesus it puts us under an obligation to forgive other people, which can be excruciatingly difficult. During the ministry time at our monthly Saturday Celebration I noticed the Holy Spirit resting upon a young woman. She had walked to the front of the church and stood silently weeping. My wife Mary and I asked her to tell us what she felt was happening. The young woman was in her late twenties, married, with young children. She confided that her marriage was strained and she was finding it increasingly difficult to give in the relationship. However, her immediate distress was related to her father. When the Holy Spirit came she felt as if she had to forgive him, but she could not do so. I asked her if she wanted to. She replied that she did, so we started to pray again. Immediately a tremendous struggle ensued within her. We encouraged her to speak out 'Dad, in Jesus' name I forgive you', but her lips seemed unable to form the words. By now an hour had passed and we took her to the large wooden cross behind the Communion Table. Standing together, I asked her to place her hands around the upright of the cross and in Jesus' name forgive her father. I have rarely witnessed such an internal battle as that which ensued during the next few minutes. All Mary and I could do was pray quietly as we called upon the Lord. Eventually, absolutely exhausted, she whispered the words of forgiveness. It was as if a steel prison door had been sprung open.

The following month we met her again. When she spoke

to us, I could not initially place her as her face and deportment had changed so much. She told us that in the intervening month her marriage had been healed in ways she could never have envisaged.

Often children need to forgive the actions of their parents. Ruth never mentioned to us why she needed to forgive her father and in such circumstances I never probe. However, for some people it is important in their healing that they actually speak out what the hurt is.

In some circumstances, continual forgiving is an important aspect of our healing. A young victim of incest I ministered to had great difficulty in coming to terms with what her father had subjected her to. She found that one prayer of forgiveness did little to alleviate the growing anger which she felt towards him. However, it was a start and we encouraged her to continue forgiving until there was nothing left to forgive.

The word 'forgiveness' literally means 'release'. As a direct result of Jesus' death on the cross the Father forgives and accepts me. This means that I am released from His judgment and my feelings of guilt. His forgiveness of me is the basis upon which I forgive others. The Apostle Paul exhorts us in this manner: 'Be kind and compassionate to one another, forgiving each other, just as in Christ God forgave you' (Ephesians 4:32).

Through an attitude of unforgiveness we bind people to ourselves through feelings of anger and resentment. When we forgive we not only release our enemies from the results of their wrong actions towards us, but also free ourselves from destructive emotions.

Holding an attitude of unforgiveness is a strong contributory factor in mental and family breakdown as well as many psychological and physical illnesses. At the end of a meeting we were leading in New Zealand, a man struggled forward for prayer. Although only in his late thirties, he was severely handicapped by swollen joints. He told us that he had first become aware of the condition three years previously and since then it had gradually worsened. This happened to be the same time as his wife had become a Christian.

In the first excitement of knowing Jesus, his wife may not have been as thoughtful towards him as she might have been and he had taken a violent dislike to her new-found faith and friends. This situation caused a barrier between them which eventually became insurmountable. He felt as if his wife was having an affair and that her love and affection had gone elsewhere. Prior to that evening he had been unable to forgive his wife or the people she associated with from the church. However, as he spoke with us, it became apparent that he wanted to put the relationship right and to trust in Jesus himself.

As we pointed him towards the cross and he called out to Jesus for mercy, the Holy Spirit came upon him in such power that we were unable to hold him up and he crumpled on to the floor. About an hour later he came to talk with me, bringing his wife with him. They appeared so happy together. All the swelling in his joints had gone and with it the continuous pain. God's forgiveness to him and to his wife and her friends had released a powerful healing in his body.

Forgiveness in our families is so important in seeking to live in love and peace with each other. The problem of being a parent is that it is impossible to have a re-run of our parenthood. When our children are small we are too busy looking after them to find time to read books which could help us in this most demanding task. It is only much later that we receive helpful insights and then it is often too late to implement them. Looking back on the way I have related to my own children, I am conscious of the many situations in which I should have acted differently had I been able. Unfortunately we are all affected in some way by the mistakes of our own parents.

With my eldest son I had in my mind a prototype of the person he should be. The standards I set for him were much higher than I would have ever set for myself. This meant that from his early years I disciplined him in an irrational way. Obviously discipline is an important feature of any child's development, but irrational discipline is harmful and creates rebellion and anger within the child. I had unattainable expectations of him.

For many years I thought that the periodic problems in our relationship stemmed from his stubbornness. However, I eventually realised that my expectations of him were the real problem. One evening, as we talked together, I told him I was sorry for the ways in which I had often made his life difficult through my unreasonable demands. This allowed him the opportunity to express his own frustrations. It was then that I asked him to forgive me for the times I had hurt him. My acknowledgment of my faults released our relationship into a new dimension.

An Indian bishop friend of mine visited England and lived for a few weeks with a Christian family. He was overwhelmed with his host's goodness and hospitality, but he confided in me that he was concerned that his host never had family prayers. This had surprised him as, in his culture, the Christian family would always assemble at a prescribed time each day and, after reading the Scriptures, spend time in prayer.

When Mary and I married we decided that this would be the pattern for our family. Such commitment was relatively easy whilst our three children were under eleven, but in early teenage years it became progressively more difficult. I believed that Christian families should pray together, and I insisted that we did so. Unfortunately, instead of creating an atmosphere of love and faith within our family, it stirred up resentment and rebellion.

I also insisted that they always attended church and took an active part in the various youth activities. At times they would complain and rebel but I never listened to what may have been legitimate complaints.

As parents we can so easily blame our children for their unreasonableness, whereas it is often we who are being unreasonable. Again, as the truth of the situation dawned upon me, I sought their forgiveness for my unreasonableness and freed them to make their own choices.

In our daily lives we need to be continually releasing forgiveness to those who we feel have hurt us by their attitudes or actions. Often this can be for the most seemingly trivial thing but, if it is not immediately dealt with, it will fester. Recently I telephoned Directory Enquiries, asking for a number. I gave the town, the name of the person, and the road in which they lived. The operator then asked for the name of the house or road number. I told her that I did not have that information. She replied that she would not give me the number unless I did. Initially I thought she was joking but soon realised that she was in earnest. Having established that she had found the person I was wanting, I further tried to coax her into giving me the number, but she adamantly refused.

As we spoke I felt anger rising and I wanted to tell her exactly how I viewed her at that moment. However, I know from past experience that my anger does not facilitate the work of the Holy Spirit so I said I was sorry that she felt she could not give the number, and rang off. I was subsequently given it by another operator.

Jesus teaches that God's forgiveness of us is dependent upon our forgiving those who hurt us. Forgiving the telephone operator was not a big deal, although I knew that I had to do it immediately otherwise I would brood over her attitude and continue to feel angry. However, there are situations which are not as easily resolved as that one. These concern relationships in which a person continues to be offensive.

We have friends who moved into their Hampstead council flat in 1980. They occupied the two top floors, whereas a retired couple lived on the ground floor. The flats were connected by a communal stairway. From the first day the occupants of the ground floor flat took exception to Peter and Joyce. The husband complained that they were too noisy on the stairs, and played music and talked too loudly in their flat. To maintain peace our friends wore slippers whilst indoors and tiptoed on the stairs yet still this did not placate them. Forgiveness was an attitude which Peter and Joyce had to maintain for nearly eight years. At times the situation drove them to distraction, and often they thought of leaving, but there were no options open to them in that direction. Regularly they prayed for the couple and asked the Lord to break through the apparent impasse. One day they saw an ambulance arrive and rush the husband off to the intensive care unit of the local hospital. He had suffered a severe heart attack. Peter visited and asked his neighbour to forgive him anything that stood between them. The old man wept as he held Peter's hand.

Another Peter, one of Jesus' followers, had problems in such situations. He was prepared to forgive but only in a limited way, after which he would cut himself off from the person concerned. He had landed on an arbitrary figure of 'seven' times. Jesus multiplied this figure by seventy, implying that forgiveness must be without limit. Whilst Peter was trying to work out the implications of such a statement, Jesus told him a simple story about two debtors. The first one owed his employer a considerable amount of money which he had no possibility of repaying. When asked to settle his debt, he cast himself upon the mercy of his employer who, moved with compassion, cancelled all that was owed him. The man bounded out of his employer's office as if the weight of the whole world had been taken off his shoulders. As he left he was met by a minor official who owed him a relatively small sum. Instead of handing on the mercy which he had received, he had the official imprisoned until he had paid all his debt. When the employer heard what had happened, he was furious and demanded that the first man be put in prison until he had paid the debt which had previously been cancelled. Jesus added a postscript to this story, reminding Peter that his heavenly Father would treat similarly all who do not forgive from their heart.

Richard and Joanna had been married five years when they encountered apparently insurmountable problems in their relationship. During their courtship Joanna had become pregnant. In the panic of the moment they decided upon an abortion. It was shortly after this trauma that they both became Christians and consequently started to sort out their lives with Jesus. They had confessed the wrongness of this action and both knew that, through Jesus, they had been forgiven. At the same time Joanna had forgiven Richard yet it transpired that, in all their arguments, it was always the abortion which she held against him. As we talked together she realised that her forgiveness of Richard had only been in words.

When Jesus uses the term 'heart', He is referring not only to the source of our will, but also to our emotions. Joanna had been deeply hurt by the abortion. This had resulted in many emotions being trapped. It was only as she expressed her real feelings of anger and resentment that the Holy Spirit was able to release her into an attitude of true forgiveness. When we do not forgive from the heart we are harbouring within us a destructive power.

At the early morning church gathering for prayer I had a picture which illustrates what happens to us when we do forgive. In my mind I saw a saddle. It reminded me of my teenage years when I used to ride horses. One of the more onerous jobs associated with riding is regularly treating the tackle. The leather saddle needs washing with saddle soap and oiling. If this discipline is neglected, the saddle becomes dry, then hard, and finally cracks.

When we fail to forgive we quickly dry up spiritually because God's forgiveness of us is dependent upon us forgiving others. Then comes a hardness of spirit, during which we become critical and condemning of others. Finally, we crack. In extreme instances some people's illness, both physical and psychological, has its origin in a spirit of unforgiveness. If they had decided to forgive then a healing process could have started immediately.

Forgiveness is part of a much wider spiritual battle being fought in the hearts and lives of men and women. We as Christians have an enemy, the Devil, and he will do all in his power to keep us locked in an attitude of unforgiveness. He will appeal to our pride and offer us every excuse not to forgive a person who has wronged us. His appeal will concentrate on the hurt we feel and the probable reception we would receive if we were to make the first step in reconciliation. Above all he knows that unforgiveness will separate us from God. He is well aware of the truth of what Jesus taught when He said, 'If you forgive men when they sin against you, your heavenly Father will also forgive you. But if you do not forgive men their sins, your Father will not forgive your sins' (Matthew 6:14–15).

Jesus has stated categorically that the Father will not forgive the unforgiving. The implications of this are serious and far-reaching. It means that, into eternity, an unforgiving attitude will separate a person for ever from the presence of God. By such an attitude a person is rejecting the great sacrifice which God has made on the cross – a sacrifice which enables forgiveness to flow through Christ into the lives of believers and, through them, into the world. Unforgiveness blocks this process and makes a mockery of Christ's death for the sin of man.

Chapter 5

DRIVING OUT EVIL

It has been my privilege to visit and minister in Sri Lanka on a number of occasions but one incident, in particular, is for ever etched on my memory. Although the day in question dawned bright, the atmosphere became heavier and the sky turned a dark shade of grey as it progressed. That evening we were leading a meeting in Colombo at the Cathedral of the Holy Spirit. As we travelled to our venue the darkness and oppressiveness increased and it became as night.

Halfway through the celebration a most terrifying storm erupted above the cathedral. The cracks of thunder resounded around the dome and flashes of lightning momentarily lit up everything with a pure white light. A deluge of rain followed and torrents of water swirled down the surrounding roads and brought all traffic to a halt. The weather office summarised our experience as being the result of cold and warm fronts colliding: an apt picture of another aspect of the cross.

When Jesus started His anointed ministry the Devil opposed Him. Initially, in the wilderness of Judea, and then as He started His public preaching in the synagogue at Capernaum (Mark 1:21), Jesus' special friend John summarised his Master's ministry in this way: 'The reason the Son of God appeared was to destroy the devil's work' (1 John 3:8). Subsequently, a large part of what Jesus did involved setting people free who were oppressed or possessed by unclean spirits. The Apostle Peter reminded Cornelius, a Roman Officer, of this aspect of Jesus' work. He told how

'God anointed Jesus of Nazareth with the Holy Spirit and power and how he went around doing good and healing all who were under the power of the devil' (Acts 10:38).

There was a gradual build-up of hostility against Jesus which reached its climax in His death. Besides the human opposition assembled to ridicule Him, so also came the demonic. Satan and the demons gathered around the cross thinking that they were witnessing the ultimate death of the Son of God. No wonder we are told that darkness came upon the land from midday until Christ died. During this time the cross became the centre of the cosmos as the Kingdom of God collided with the kingdom of darkness. As Jesus died there was a violent earthquake which split rocks open. The enormous curtain in the Temple, which separated the people from the most holy place, was torn from top to bottom. Dead people were seen to come back to life.

This moment of apparent disaster was in fact the moment of incredible victory. Satan's misuse of power had come through his disobedience whereas by His perfect obedience even to death on the cross Jesus had broken Satan's power over the lives of men and women. He had become victor, as His resurrection proclaimed to the world of men and devils.

Like many ministers of my generation, I studied theology at a conservative evangelical college. Here I learnt that demons appeared in the first century to oppose Jesus as He sought to establish God's Kingdom. However, it was vaguely assumed that today the Church did not expect such phenomena as it was well and truly established. Reading Scripture, I could never be really convinced of the perception. Here we meet a Jesus who is not only casting out demons on many occasions, but also authorising His followers to do the same in His name. However, I had never had any experience to cause me to think about it seriously until one evening at St Andrew's vicarage.

During the early sixties I belonged to a group which met there regularly on a Friday evening. This meeting started late, which allowed commuters time with their families before joining us. The format of the evening consisted of a time of sharing followed by worship and prayer. On this particular occasion there was a lady present who had practised as a spiritist's medium. When she turned to Christ she repented and renounced this evil practice.

At the sharing time that evening she told how she was constantly harassed by evil and violent thoughts. As she was speaking it occurred to me that her problem was an evil spirit. This was the first time I had ever thought in this way. In those days people in the circles in which I moved never talked about such things. Nobody present made any comment except John, the vicar, who suggested that we pray.

From my seat I found myself commanding the evil spirit to go, in the name of Jesus. I had hardly spoken the words when the lady concerned screwed up her body and I saw on her shoulder the most grotesque-looking, animal-like creature I have ever seen. It appeared to be about eighteen inches long, furry and with a long tail. At my second mention of Jesus' name it fled through the door. Needless to say, I was much taken aback by what happened. However, as I pursued this phenomenon further, I realised that Jesus spoke of driving demons out of people as being a sign of the presence and power of His Kingdom.

On another occasion a young man, who had only been a Christian for a few months, came one Sunday evening after the service and asked for prayer. I had prayed with him previously for an anxiety state. It seemed as if, instead of gradual improvement which I should have expected, his condition worsened. After inviting the Holy Spirit to minister to him, he started to shake and his face distorted. I perceived the presence of evil and sensed that the Lord was going to drive it out. Taking the authority of the cross and speaking in the name of Jesus, I commanded all evil to leave him. He recalled afterwards that it was as if a powerful force entered his head and swept right through his body. Whilst this happened another more sinister presence left through his feet. Having seen the power of evil manifested in this way, the temptation is to explain every psychological, emotional, spiritual and physical disorder in terms of a demonic presence. The danger is to believe more in the Devil's power than Christ's once-and-for-all victory over him won on the cross. Reflecting on this victory Paul stated that Jesus: 'Disarmed the powers and authorities, he made a public spectacle of them, triumphing over them by the cross' (Colossians 2:15). The Christian does not believe in the Devil, rather he believes in the Lord Jesus Christ and the effect of His victory over all evil.

Much harm has been done by people who see devils in every situation. I know of a number of people who have been prayed with and told that their problem was due to the presence of a devil. After a seemingly authoritative prayer has been said over them, they have returned home only to find that their problem is still with them. This has given rise to the false belief that they are still demonised. Others have suffered in even more distressing ways when they have screamed out during worship. People have then tried, over a lengthy period, to cast a demon out of them whereas their real problem has been emotional. It can take many months of sympathetic counselling to help back to normality a person who has been traumatised in this way. However, there is a small minority of situations where demonisation is the only explanation and the cross of Jesus the only answer.

In my experience I started to see that at times physical conditions could be the result of the person being demonised. This was certainly the case with a crippled woman to whom Jesus ministered healing (Luke 13:10). He had met her in a worship service. For eighteen years she had been bent over and was unable to straighten her body at all. Jesus perceived that her condition was the result of a spirit which had demonised her. With a word He immediately set her free from her condition and she straightened up. Again, a man who was unable to talk was brought to Jesus. From this man He drove out a demon, after which he was able to talk normally (Matthew 9:33). There was also the experience of a blind man who saw immediately the demon had left (Matthew 12:22).

I was ministering in Holland with a small team. At the conclusion of our first meeting I was called over to a group who were praying for a young woman. She was sitting and shaking all over with cold, although the evening was warm. I asked her what she thought was causing her distress. She replied that whenever she welcomed the Holy Spirit, her teeth chattered and her body became cold and shook. She then told me this story.

Nine months previously she had been on holiday in the Greek city of Thessalonica. One day whilst walking through the market-place, she heard someone preaching about Jesus being alive. She had never heard the Gospel before and, after listening to the young man for some time, stayed on to talk with him. He explained to her she could receive Christ and then offered to pray. As she invited Christ into her life, she experienced an intense flow of energy into her chest. Knowing Christ brought her great joy and on returning to Holland she joined the fellowship at the church where we were.

However, her joy was short-lived as she became ill. For the next nine months she suffered from attacks of bronchitis and asthma, two conditions which she never previously had. This had left her weak and resulted in her spending long periods in bed. As she talked I sensed that her condition might have something to do with her childhood so I asked her to share what she could remember of her early years. It transpired that her parents' marriage ended when she was four or five. She stayed with her mother until she was eight and then they moved abroad. After a period of time she was sent back to her father. He was angry at her unannounced arrival and while she stayed he was cruel and violent to her. Eventually she was put in the care of foster parents who also beat her.

It is my observation that a demonic presence can attach itself to a child at the moment of a traumatic experience. Whilst she was recounting these things to me, I sensed that she had a spirit of infirmity which had been stirred up when she accepted Christ. I rebuked it in Jesus' name and told her to breathe deeply. As she did so, her chest extended and filled with air in a way that had been impossible previously. The following day she was due to have an extensive examination at the hospital. Subsequently she came late to the meeting with the exciting news that the hospital had given her a clean bill of health.

If it is possible that through a particularly traumatic childhood experience the Devil can gain a foothold in a person's life; it can also happen through a person's persistent involvement in the occult. Scripture especially forbids and warns us against the result of such practices. 'Let no one be found among you who sacrifices his son or daughter in the fire, who practises divination or sorcery, interprets omens, engages in witchcraft, or casts spells, or who is a medium or spiritist, or who consults the dead. Anyone who does these things is detestable to the Lord' (Deuteronomy 18:10–12).

When an unclean spirit leaves a person it causes a spiritual vacuum which must be filled immediately. Jesus describes the condition in this way. 'When an evil spirit comes out of a man, it goes through arid places seeking rest and does not find it. Then it says "I will return to the house I left." When it arrives, it finds the house unoccupied, swept clean and put in order. Then it goes and takes with it seven other spirits more wicked than itself, and they go in and live there. And the final condition of that man is worse than the first' (Matthew 12:43–45).

As Christians we are temples of the Holy Spirit and when He is fully in the temple there is no room left for other spirits. This certainly became the young woman's experience as the power of God filled the vacuum created by the departing spirit.

In the early days of my ministry in Cornwall I met a young man from Nigeria. Peter was sponsored by his government and was studying at the Camborne School of Mines. Our family befriended him and we found his openness to spiritual matters a continual source of inspiration and encouragement. However, after about six months he started to behave in rather odd ways. He claimed to be receiving messages from God and his interpretation of the Scriptures became quite bizarre.

I tried to talk with him about what was happening, but it became increasingly difficult to have a rational conversation. He told me that he had received a message from God to the effect that a family in Nigeria had put a curse on him. According to him this had been confirmed by a letter which he had received from his village. Peter was of average height and weight, supple and well-built. Suddenly he started to lose weight. The lady he lodged with became concerned and visited me. It transpired that he had not eaten for three weeks.

In vain I tried to reason with him. He said that God had told him the only way the curse could be broken was if he fasted. We watched helplessly as he took to his bed and grew progressively weaker. The local doctor and I prayed regularly, but he remained under the influence of what he thought was a curse. He eventually deteriorated to such an extent that his government flew him home. I have heard nothing of him since.

It raised many questions. Was Peter's condition self-induced? Had he simply convinced himself that he was cursed and acted upon it, or had sinister spiritual forces been at work? Was the letter from his village a coincidence, or did the witch doctor have a special insight? Why was prayer, in the name of Jesus, seemingly so ineffective?

About the same time I came into contact with a couple who had recently returned from South America, where the husband had been involved in a mining business. They had prospered and bought one of the largest houses in a prominently working-class town. I met them as a result of the husband asking me to visit his wife. She was a lady in her late fifties who was suffering from an acute form of arthritis which affected most of her joints. She talked at length about her crippling disease which had apparently started without warning a few years previously. Understanding that this condition could be brought about by a traumatic event or unresolved emotional problems, I questioned her about such possibilities, but drew a blank. However, she did remember something that had happened about the time she first became conscious of swollen joints.

One morning, whilst collecting the milk from the gate, she noticed something on the lawn. On closer examination she found it to be a doll made out of white calico. Its face had been embroidered and there were red dots on all its joints; through these, pins had been pushed. She subsequently thought that either a servant from South America or a local person, motivated by jealousy, had put a curse on her. Again, my prayers seemed to be ineffective.

These instances happened nearly twenty years ago and since then I have been involved with similar situations which I now know to be the result of curses. We read in the early history of Israel that, on their way to the Promised Land, the Israelites defeated the Amorites in battle after which they laid siege to Moab. Balak, the Moabite king, was terrified and sent envoys to Babylon for help. It was here that Balaam lived. He was a professional diviner, soothsayer and prophet. Balak sought to employ him to put a curse on Israel. In this particular instance the Lord intervened and He would not allow such a curse to rest upon His people. However, there are certainly situations when such an occult curse does seem to have a devastating and destructive effect. I notice that a curse can also be put upon a person by another, through negative words spoken over them.

Mary and I were asked to lead an evening at an Oxford college. After we had spoken we ministered in the power of the Holy Spirit, and during this time we prayed with a young woman. She had a physical problem which emanated from her right shoulder into her back. I asked her when the condition had started; what she described was not uncommon in our experience.

Sharon's mother was severely crippled with an arthritic condition which had made her an invalid for most of her married life. Ever since Sharon could remember she had been told that there was a fifty per cent chance that she would inherit her mother's condition. Recent medical opinion had confirmed her worst suspicions; she now had her mother's disease.

Having invoked the Holy Spirit to come in the name of Jesus, we put His cross between Sharon and her mother. With a prayer we broke the power of the expectation of disease which had come upon her. The power of God came upon Sharon and she shook before collapsing on to the floor. After ten minutes she tried to stand, but was unable and staggered into a chair like a drunken person. For the first time she was completely without pain and was overjoyed by the feelings of release and freedom.

There is a petition in the Lord's Prayer where we ask that our heavenly Father will deliver us from evil, and He hears that prayer. But sometimes we meet people who have deliberately given themselves over to the pursuit of evil, and can exercise its power against us.

Beverly is a physiotherapist attached to a large hospital. She attended a conference at our church and at the end of one of the sessions asked me if I would pray with her. The previous Wednesday she had a strange experience with one of her patients. The lady concerned arrived in the treatment rooms, said 'hallo' and then sat and stared at Beverly, who felt as if she was in the presence of an incredible evil. Fear overcame her, her stomach became knotted and she had an overwhelming sensation of sickness. Excusing herself, she went into the staff room where she was physically sick. Even after three days she was still fearful and felt as if, in some way, she had been defiled.

Jesus taught that anyone who followed Him could be filled with the Holy Spirit. Such a filling always results in the believer radiating something of the nature of Jesus, which is love. At times this can be an awe-inspiring experience. In our church and in my travels I have often met people in whose presence I have sensed wonderful love and acceptance. The opposite is also true. If a person opens his life to the things of Satan, then he can be filled with his evil nature. The woman

Beverly met would have fitted into this latter category. As a Christian, Beverly was particularly sensitive to the presence of evil. Planting the cross between Beverly and the woman concerned, I broke all powers and evil influences. Beverly was immediately filled with peace and the Holy Spirit.

The Apostle Paul understood the Christian life in terms of a spiritual wrestling match (Ephesians 6:10). He intimated that in this match the adversary motivated people to oppose and destroy the people of God. It is in this context that the Christian discovers the power of the name of Jesus to overcome evil.

Whilst teaching in the Youth With A Mission school in Madras the leader, Tim, shared with me the following incident. With Carol, his wife, and their two young daughters they were travelling by train for a holiday in Kashmir, a state in northern India. This journey took them through the central Indian state of Madhya Pradesh and lasted three days and nights. This particular state is notorious for its highway bandits.

On the morning of the second day Carol was seeking the Lord in prayer when she felt as if the Lord was indicating to her that she and the family needed to be particularly vigilant that evening. She remembered praying at length for Tim and the girls. When evening came the family, with others in their compartment, settled down to sleep. Tim, by nature, is a deep sleeper and, according to his family, nothing disturbs him once he has dropped off. This night was to be different. At about 10.00 p.m. he suddenly awoke and sat bolt upright. In his sleep he had heard a child's voice calling 'Daddy'. In a split second he realised that his eldest daughter was in the hands of kidnappers. As he launched himself into the corridor he bound the powers of evil in the name of Jesus. At this moment he was particularly aware of the power of the Holy Spirit upon him.

Outside the train door he saw his daughter in the arms of a man who had obviously received her from a group within. Forcing his way to the door he grabbed his daughter and

fought with the man who was trying to abduct her. Within
seconds he had her back in his arms and into the safety of
the compartment.

This particular state is a centre for child prostitution and
pornography. The gang had waited at a place where the train
slowed down for a bend. On boarding they had lifted the
sleeping child. The man outside intended to jump with her
from the slow moving train. If this had happened she probably
would have disappeared for ever.

To the Christians at Ephesus (Ephesians 6:10), Paul wrote
about 'the devil's schemes' (v.11) which confronts us 'on the
day of evil' (v.13). These attacks come like 'flaming arrows
of the evil one' (v.16). A flaming arrow is an apt description
of his assault on our minds. It reminds me of the old cowboy
and Indian movies. In most scenes, before they are routed
in defeat, the Indians surround the wagons and fire arrows
into them with lighted feathers attached. When these penetrate
a wagon it almost immediately becomes a blaze.

From Matthew's account of the temptation of Jesus
(Matthew 4:1) it would seem that these occurred in His mind
and involved His imagination. We read that '. . . the devil
took him to the holy city, and had him stand on the highest
point' (v.5), and again '. . . the devil took him to a very high
mountain, and showed him all the kingdoms of the world and
their splendour' (v.8).

I include the following personal experience in order that
it may be of help to some. On one occasion I was in my study
praying. During this time I felt as if the Lord was asking me
to dedicate myself to Him in a fresh way. As I sought to
respond He asked me to surrender my wife Mary to Him,
and then our two young children. As I did this my heart
started to pound at an incredible rate; I shook from head to
toe. He then told me He was taking my life. These words
brought a fear which seemed to explode in my mind. I felt
as if I was dying when suddenly my study was filled with a
dazzling light, the brightness of which I had never seen before
or since. For many months this experience unsettled me as

I tried to make sense of it. Eventually, I came to the conclusion
that it was a devilish attack. I had allowed the 'flaming arrow'
into my mind. In fact I had been deceived by the voice which
I thought to be the Lord's. Twenty years later I was reading
John White's excellent best-selling book entitled *When the Spirit
Comes with Power*. In his chapter entitled 'Stolen Power' he
describes an almost identical experience which he had during
a week of prayer and fasting. At the end of a most frightening
experience he realised that it was the Devil.

One of the most powerful desires in all of us is sexual. In
a loving, committed marriage relationship this can reach
heights of beauty and creativity. Equally, it can hurt, damage
and destroy. It is an area in which all are vulnerable, and
in which the Devil seeks to wreak havoc. For the single person
the temptation is to fornicate, whereas for the married it is
to commit adultery. Both of these acts start in the mind, when
we realise that we are being physically attracted to someone
of the opposite sex.

Once a man telephoned me who seemed to be in great
distress. However, he would not discuss anything on the
telephone, but wanted to make an appointment to see me.
When we eventually met I discovered that he was happily
married with a young family. During our introductory
conversation, I realised that he was an excellent sportsman
and, from the senior management position he held, he must
have been promoted well above his years.

Two years previously he and his wife had become Christians
and consequently were taking an active role in their local
church. Eventually, and very hesitantly, he introduced the
matter for which he had come. In his job he travelled
extensively and had recently been to a conference based in
a well-known London hotel. He had had a demanding day
lecturing and meeting many new people. He took a late supper
and then went to the bar for a drink before retiring. It was
here that he met a most attractive young woman who had
also been a delegate at the conference. They talked together
until everyone had left the room except the staff. By this time

they had become emotionally drawn to each other, and as they had rooms on the same floor, they were playfully suggesting that they should share one together. It was at this moment that he suddenly realised what he was about to do. In panic, he excused himself and rushed to his room.

Subsequently he had been full of guilt and remorse; he was finding a barrier developing in his relationship with his wife. He was not sleeping and at work he had become short-tempered with his staff. He looked at me disbelievingly when I told him that such temptations were common to all men, and often more especially to Christians. He asked me to explain what I meant.

I told him that we could not help the devilish temptations any more than Jesus could (Hebrews 4:15) but our responsibility was what we did with them. If we fail to stop the lustful thoughts entering the front door of our minds, then we must quickly push them straight out the back door before they lead to action. In this skirmish with the Devil, he had obviously been wounded. After his confession I rebuked the enemy and welcomed the Holy Spirit afresh upon him. Consequently he was to tell me that the temptations still came in that area, but by God's grace he was seeking to resist and walk away from them.

In this whole area of the spiritual battle, an incident in which I was involved helped me to understand more fully the authority that Jesus has given over the enemy. My parents-in-law had moved from a bungalow to a town house just off the High Street in a Hampshire town renowned as a yachting centre. The house had a garage which was in a row with six others. It also had a numbered plot in the forecourt where a car could be parked if not garaged.

When we first visited I parked our car on the small plot. We had hardly stepped out of the car when we were assailed by an elderly woman wielding a stick and pushing a shopping trolley. What, she demanded to know, was I doing parking my car on this particular forecourt? Her opening remark was followed by condemnation of others, like myself, who had parked cars there illegally.

I eventually told her I was visiting a house on the estate. Icily, she demanded to know which one. Counting to ten slowly, I gave her the name of the person and the number of the house.

On reflection I realised that I had no authority myself whatsoever to do what I did. However, my authority was given me by my father-in-law who had sole right to the piece of land. He was able to give authority to whoever he liked. In the same way I have no authority or power of my own on the spiritual battlefield yet I have, with all Christians, the authority of Jesus to drive out demons and to walk over all the power of the enemy. This authority is firmly based in the victory over Satan which Jesus won on the cross. From what can be gleaned from the Old Testament it would seem that Satan tried to usurp God's position and, as a result, was cast out of heaven and divested of the authority under God which he had enjoyed. At the creation God gave man authority over all the created world. However, through his disobedience, which was instigated by Satan, he forfeited this and Satan assumed it. One of the major results of this was that Satan misused the spiritual power given to man, for destructive purposes. He consequently locked mankind into a cycle of disobedience. The way that Jesus could wrest this authority from him was by perfect obedience and this culminated on the cross where He '. . . became obedient to death – even death on a cross! Therefore God exalted him to the highest place' (Philippians 2:8–9).

Chapter 6

'OF COURSE I DO'

Jesus not only healed people from demonic influences but He also healed the physically and emotionally sick. Reflecting on His death, Matthew concluded that on the cross Jesus '. . . took up our infirmities and carried our diseases' (Matthew 8:17). There is healing power from the cross.

I will always remember my first visit to Calcutta Cathedral for two reasons. The evening meetings started at 5.30 p.m., just as those who work in that great city were travelling home. The exhaust fumes from cars, buses and lorries combined with the dust and stench to form a grey cloud which hung head high above the city. This made our throats so sore that we had to wear handkerchiefs across our faces, reminiscent of American cowboys.

In India there are always vast crowds at such meetings and this night was no exception. After a period of worship, I spoke on the power of the cross to heal. When I had finished I invited those who would like prayer to kneel at the Communion rail. Whilst people were responding I noticed a Bengali woman walking forward to where I was standing. I was taken aback by her appearance. Her face was like that of a skeleton, as were her hands and forearms. Beneath a colourful sari her stomach protruded as if she were pregnant. Bishop Bairagi of Barrackpore, who was interpreting for me, said that she was in the last stages of cancer. I placed my hands on her abdomen and asked, in Jesus' name, that He would heal her. She was in severe pain, as drugs are only available for the rich and she was poor. As soon as we prayed she experienced an immediate loss of pain and a feeling of heat through her body. After the meeting she disappeared with her friends into the crowds. This happened in 1983.

In 1985 our church hosted a conference for church leaders from twenty-two different countries. As I arrived for the first meeting I was greeted in the car park by Bishop Bairagi. He proceeded to tell me a wonderful story. Prior to visiting England he was paying a pastoral visit to one of his parishes when he was met by an excited woman. Until she related her story, he had no idea who she was. She introduced herself as Provabati, the cancer-ridden lady we had prayed for in the Cathedral. She said that during the prayer she felt waves of intense heat flow through her body. On returning to her home she found that, instead of continuing to lose strength, she gained it. After a few weeks there was a noticeable shrinking of her grossly distended abdomen. The pain, which had become almost unbearable, receded to an occasional ache. She had returned to the weight she had been before the onset of the disease.

In 1987 I returned to Calcutta with a small team. For three evenings we ministered in Christ Church, Dum Dum. Dum Dum is a suburb of Calcutta which is better known for its British military associations than its church. On the second evening Provabati attended the meeting with her husband. I invited her to share with the congregation what the Lord had done in her life. She proved to be exceptionally eloquent. Those who listened were spell-bound as she described the onset of the cancer and the suffering that ensued. This was particularly poignant as there were many who had observed the decline she was describing.

When she eventually finished, I spoke. Scrapping the notes I had previously made, I told the people that it was through Jesus and the power of His cross that she stood healed before them. I then offered them Christ, inviting those who did not know Him to come to the front of the meeting. A holy hush fell upon the gathering as between eighty and a hundred filed forward.

Some would argue that miraculous healings which are recorded in the New Testament Scriptures are confined to the ministry of Jesus and the early Christians. Yet this position is difficult to maintain in the light of Christian history and contemporary experience. Those who have sought to minister healing in the name of Jesus have taken their authority to do so from His commission and the healing power released from the cross.

At the heart of the Old Testament prophecies stands the fifty-third chapter of Isaiah where, through the inspiration of the Holy Spirit, the prophet vividly sees the sufferings and death of the Messiah. The effect of this death is first and foremost to make an atonement for the sin of mankind. 'But he was pierced for our transgressions, he was crushed for our iniquities; the punishment that brought us peace was upon him' (v.5). This means that through the Messiah's sacrifice the wrath of God is turned away and He is reconciled to man. It also means that within the huge cosmic scope of the atonement He also absorbed into His body on the cross our sickness. 'Surely he took up our infirmities and carried our sorrows' (v.4). And '. . . by his wounds we are healed' (v.5).

It is my experience that there are occasions when the power of God is particularly present to heal the sick. Luke records in chapter 5 verse 17 of his Gospel, '. . . the power of the Lord was present for him to heal the sick.' It is as if the Holy Spirit is highlighting and honouring this aspect of Jesus' work. We have encountered this especially at evangelistic meetings.

Before Alastair Forman became vicar of St Hughes, Lewsey, he and his wife Alison pastored St Saviour's, Brookwood, a church in Woking. Alastair invited us to bring a team to his church. We had an encouraging first week, based on people's homes, and during the second led a series of 'God in Action' evenings in the church.

At the first meeting I was speaking on the healing of the paralytic by Peter and John, as recorded in Acts chapter 3. In preparation it had occurred to me that the gifts of the Spirit were clearly in evidence in this act of God.

Peter and John were on their way to the Temple when they met a man being carried on a stretcher. He was being taken to his particular place where for many years he had begged money from the worshippers. On the stretcher he was going through his pitiful routine. Peter challenged him to look at them. As he looked up Peter perceived that he had the faith to believe. The power of miracles was evidently upon Peter and he spoke the word of faith when he said, 'In the name of Jesus Christ of Nazareth, walk.' Doctor Luke records that instantly his feet and ankles became firm.

Whilst I was expanding on this incident, I became conscious of a young lady who was sitting with one of her legs stretched out in the aisle. The knee was heavily bandaged and the leg was supported by a small stool on which her foot rested. Leaning against the seat in front of her were two aluminium crutches which she needed to enable her to walk. As I talked about this healing miracle I was so full of faith, but as I periodically glanced at this lady, I began to waver slightly. What would happen, I wondered, if she requested prayer?

After my talk we had a time of ministry, and then just what I had dreaded happened! She reached for her crutches and, with the help of friends, started hobbling forward. At the prayer ministry it is usual for our team to go and stand at the front and for those who want prayer to meet them there. By the time this lady arrived the only people not praying were Alison and myself. She told us that her name was Judith and that, over a period of six years, she had undergone six operations to try to overcome the problem of a worn-out knee cap. All these operations were unsuccessful and eventually the surgeon removed the knee cap. Even this drastic step did not help and she suffered continuous pain which could not be alleviated by drugs. For the last two years, however, friends had prayed for her regularly.

As we prayed and Alison asked the Holy Spirit to come and to heal her, Judith records that she felt Him come upon her and, as prayer continued, God's power increased and a tremendous heat went right through her leg. Suddenly she fell to the ground, 'resting' in the Spirit. Alison stayed with her and I moved on to pray with others.

A loud cry went up from the congregation. I looked up to see Judith walking down the aisle, unaided and without crutches. People were clapping and cheering. I noticed that she was still heavily bandaged and, even though there was much rejoicing, I did not at that moment have the faith to tell her to take the bandages off.

The next evening we arrived an hour early so that we could pray before the meeting. A number were already there, including Judith. She was without her crutches, bandages, or foot rest. We began the evening with our customary forty minutes of worship, and then Alastair invited testimonies from the congregation. Judith was the first on her feet. She told us about her day, which she had started by going shopping in Guildford with her mother. This had caused many shopkeepers to ask questions. They had become accustomed to seeing her heavily bandaged and on crutches. They asked her what had happened to cause the change, and she was able to tell them exactly what Jesus had done for her.

After lunch she had one of her regular check-ups at the hospital with the physiotherapist. This appointment was going to be slightly different because the consultant had made arrangements for her to be measured for a support for her damaged leg. The physiotherapist was astonished and delighted when she saw her – a reaction repeated by her consultant. However, she wrote to say that this work of God had produced very mixed reactions. Some people still refused to believe that it was God's work, whilst others stood back in amazement and wanted to know more about God's power.

The power of the cross to heal can come upon a person quite spontaneously. Janet Cornelius wrote to me recently from St Albans. She had attended a study day which the Church Pastoral Aid Society had hosted at St Luke's, Bricket Wood. I had been invited to lead this with a team. Janet had a severe form of rheumatoid arthritis. She writes that, after prayer, she was surprised to find that her knees and ankles became even more swollen and painful. However, by the morning she was free of pain and swelling.

A week went by and, whilst she was reading a book on healing, she experienced the power of God coming upon her again. For more than two hours her knees and ankles vibrated. This was to be repeated the following week. As a result she is walking freely, feeling full of energy, and has no further need of anti-inflammatory drugs. Her letter ends with a postscript in which she said that since her healing she has had a tremendous craving for knowledge of the Bible.

The power of God becomes the power to heal when faith is present.

With a small team we were with Bishop Bairagi in the northern part of his diocese of West Bengal. We had travelled from Calcutta along the Bangladesh border to Krishnanagar. The first night's meeting in the local church was slightly fraught. It started with a dog fight; eventually the contestants were coaxed into a courtyard where they continued unabated. The man on the pump at the manual organ was obviously tired and occasionally fell asleep. As soon as I rose to speak the lights went out and the fans slowed down. I waited as candles were lit and brought to the front. We had just become settled when the fans started up and blew the candles out! In such a manner the evening progressed. In the midst of this three women appeared through the darkness and walked straight to the front where I was standing with my interpreter, the Bishop. Again the meeting stopped while the Bishop listened to their story.

The women had been travelling for two days by train from a town in the north of his diocese. They had heard of the meetings from travellers who told them that a girl who suffered at least two fits a day had been healed at one of our meetings. One of the women was particularly ill and so with her friends had journeyed to be healed. The Bishop and I duly prayed. By now the lights, fans and candles had all gone out! With a sense of urgency the trio departed. Later I asked the Bishop why they had gone so quickly. He told me that a train left within the hour and they wanted to be on it. He said they had travelled with the express purpose of being healed, and having been healed, they had left. As later we sipped our sweet tea, I seemed to hear Jesus say, 'not in all Israel have I found faith such as this.'

During my early years our family lived in Piahatua, a small farming town which people usually went through rather than to. Few people suffered from stress, tension or ulcers in Piahatua. Boys of my age walked to school with bare feet, and after school put the 'gone fishing' note on the kitchen table. To my knowledge only one couple separated and divorced, and this was the subject of community gossip for years. Our milk was delivered by horse and cart, and it was here that I had my first ride in a car.

Today I live in a community which in many ways epitomises all that is happening in the wealthier sections of our society. We are just over half an hour from central London, and the majority of our earning people leave the community at 7 a.m. and return twelve hours later. During the week young children glimpse their father, if they see him at all. Mortgage repayments are colossal, with house prices well above the national average. Such an intensive existence makes many people anxious and tense. Again this is aggravated by the expectations which go with particularly highly paid jobs.

Geoff spoke with me because he was suffering from a duodenal ulcer. He reminded me of a cut-out replica which photographers use at fairs. Often the replica is of a famous person with a hole where his head should have been. The photographer invites people to stand behind the replica and put their head through the hole. The resulting photograph shows one person superimposed on another. This was Geoff.

In his job, marriage and church activities various people had put their expectations upon him, and he was not able to fulfil them. I told him that the power of the cross was such that it could break the cycles of tension and anxiety in which he had been enmeshed. As we prayed it was as if a spring, which had been compressed within his body, was suddenly released. He shuddered and shook before experiencing the peace of Jesus which passes all understanding.

As we talked afterwards Geoff appeared to be a different person. He asked how he could re-enter the situation which caused his problem and still retain the peace and healing he had received. I told him that it was only by prayer. This meant that each day he needed to cultivate a time in his busy schedule when he could talk with Jesus about his commitments. I reminded him that Jesus told us not to be anxious and invited us to 'cast our cares upon Him' because He cared for us.

Valerie Eccles is a member of St Saviour's Church, Brookwood, and wrote to me after we had ministered in her church. She reminded me of how we had prayed together in the curate's kitchen. Valerie had severe pain in her neck and down her right arm. Her G.P. had put her on a variety of pain killing drugs, but eventually admitted that he had exhausted all his resources. She was referred to a rheumatologist who gave her acupuncture, traction, more pain killers and a neck collar. This treatment didn't help and she was referred to a neurological consultant. He diagnosed scoliosis, which is a condition resulting in curvature of the spine. However, Valerie knew that underlying the physical condition was a deep anxiety.

She recalled that as we had prayed she had felt heat in her back and neck. It eventually became so intense that she had to sit down and ask for a glass of water. After the prayer she quickly cooled off, but felt quite strange. On a further examination her specialist noted that all her vertebrae were back in place. For her part she had seldom felt better or more free from pain. Here was another illustration of the power of the cross. It was this power that I evoked to break the stress situation, after which she experienced the healing presence of Jesus.

When I first met with evangelicals at an English theological college I was led to believe that we, as Christians, do not have problems relating to our past lives. It was a commonly held belief that, through coming to Christ, our old lives passed away and everything became new. This was good in theory, but in practice it meant that many hurtful emotions were suppressed, and we ceased to be real people. In fact, we became 'people of the masks'.

When Mary and I were married twenty-four years ago we brought to our marriage a great love for each other, but also many unresolved areas emanating from our past. These started to surface at the end of the first year. It was then that we had to decide whether we would continue to relate in the areas in which we felt comfortable, or whether we would allow ourselves to be vulnerable and face up to the difficulties which were surfacing.

When I was born my natural mother was unable, through circumstances, to keep me so I was placed with different foster parents until I was adopted at eighteen months. This enabled me, for the rest of my childhood to be brought up in a stable, loving home. However, some damage had already been done.

Over the years I have talked and prayed with many people who have been adopted and nearly all of them suffer from the same negative feelings about themselves. For an adopted person it is as if they had suddenly arrived on the planet from nowhere. They have no known parents, grand-parents, uncles, aunts or distant cousins. They feel completely rootless and deeply insecure. Irrespective of the circumstances surrounding an adoption there are innate feelings of rejection which go back to the initial rejection of the mother. The child wonders how she could ever have contemplated abandoning it. This feeling is increased as various people step into the mother role.

Such experiences give a person an emotional handicap which will be manifested in patterns of irrational behaviour. Such people are inclined to project their feelings of insecurity and rejection on to all their relationships. This is particularly so in the case of marriage where the couple are having to relate daily with each other. This may be one of the main contributory factors in marriage breakdown today. If we find it difficult to talk about our inner feelings then we create 'no go' areas with our partners.

One of my problems was in the area of rejection. If Mary said or did anything that touched on that area, then it would press a 'red button', and I would explode in an irrational and angry way. Often this would subsequently lead into periods of depression in which I went silent and retreated into myself. Mary's 'red buttons' were activated in the areas of insecurity and grief. She was a replacement baby. Her sister of four died through an attack of meningitis and ten months later Mary was born into a situation of unresolved grief. On occasions these feelings were so intense that they appeared almost to overwhelm her.

In those early days we discovered that our marriage could become a healing relationship if we were prepared to be vulnerable with each other. We gradually learnt to listen sympathetically to each other and to the Holy Spirit before we prayed for healing.

It was prophesied of the Messiah that He would 'bind up the broken-hearted' (Isaiah 61:1); 'heal the broken-hearted' (Psalm 147:3), and would be 'close to the broken-hearted' (Psalm 34:18). It is awe inspiring to realise that Jesus' heart was also broken through His experiences of rejection which culminated in His death on the cross. Not only from the cross does He empathise with us, but also from His death is healing power released.

To 'bind-up' the broken-hearted is an apt description of this particular type of ministry. I remember when, as a child, our town had a number of power cuts. One evening the candles had burnt out so I found a new one and cut it in half with a carving knife. Unfortunately, the blade also gashed part of my finger. My mother stopped the flow of blood, cleansed the wound, put on ointment and then bandaged the finger tightly. Although I did not feel better at the time, a healing process had started.

The healing of inner traumas is seldom, if ever, immediate. It is a transforming process which starts as the wound is opened to Jesus for healing and prayer is made. This continues as other areas, relating to the same problem, surface and are dealt with. In the case of my finger, it felt tender for many months after the accident; so it is with the deep hurts of the heart.

Healing of emotional hurts can be the key to physical healing. I often receive letters from grateful parents who, after many years of childlessness, discover that they are having a baby. The most recent I received was from a grandmother in Harrow. It concerned her daughter and son-in-law who live in Ireland. For seven years they were childless, having undergone all the appropriate tests. At one of our meetings we had prayed with them, and subsequently the daughter gave birth to a baby girl. When I read the grandmother's letter of thankfulness I remembered that Saturday night in Dublin. As the Holy Spirit had come He had revealed unresolved areas of hurt in the lives of the young couple. I had talked with them about this before praying, and the subsequent healing had cleared the way for conception to take place. This would be a normal occurrence in such situations.

One Sunday morning I was involved in praying for people at the front of the church after the service. This meant I supervised the ministry of prayer which always follows our services. A number of people had been prayed with, and the duty team left. I was just making sure everything in the sanctuary was in order when two young women approached. Sue and Jean were friends and came from the North of England. Earlier that morning they had travelled down to Chorleywood, especially for prayer. Sue was married, and Jean was a friend and neighbour. Jean had a chronic physical condition. She had constant pain emanating from the bottom of her spine and the cartilage area of both knees. The previous week she had been discharged from hospital where her consultant had conducted an examination of her knees under anaesthetic. He concluded that there was nothing physically amiss; yet the pain continued to be as intense as ever.

As Sue and I started to pray with her, the Holy Spirit

seemed to say to me that the problem was grief. We stopped our prayers and I asked her if that was so; she replied in the negative. I then asked her when the condition had started; she said that she became conscious of it two years previously. I enquired if there was any traumatic experience she had suffered around that period. Again she replied negatively. By now I was slightly bewildered. However, I suggested we continue to wait upon the Lord. During this time I felt that the Holy Spirit whispered a second time, 'It's grief'. Slightly embarrassed, I stopped the prayer and asked if she had lost, through death, anyone near to her two years previously. This time she acknowledged the death of her god-father. I asked what her relationship with him was and she told me he was like a father. I enquired whether she had ever grieved his death, to which she replied she had not.

As we prayed again I broke, in Jesus' name, the power of grief that was over her life. For the next twenty minutes the loss she felt for him was released in uncontrollable sobs. When she could cry no more I asked the Holy Spirit to come and heal her. Jean was filled with the power of God. Waves of heat, which caused her to perspire, flooded her back and knees. As the energy flowed, so the pain dispersed. Usually at the end of such healings I ask the person concerned what they had been unable to do. Jean said the obvious: she had been unable to bend her back or knees. Sue and I praised the Lord as Jean went through a gymnastic routine. She jogged out of the church to start her long journey home.

It is only in the context of the death of Christ that we can start to understand something of the mystery of healing and of suffering. Jesus fulfilled the prophecy of Isaiah when, on the cross, He 'took up our infirmities and carried our sorrows' (Isaiah 53:4). However, there are those situations of sickness when there is faith, expectancy and a manifestation of the Holy Spirit, yet no apparent healing takes place.

My friend Iain Roberts, to whom this book is dedicated, died of cancer. He was a most remarkable man. He founded the neurological unit at the Central Middlesex Hospital and for many years was, nationally, a leading consultant in his field. Some years ago he was invited by the publishers to re-edit the standard work on neurosurgery. As well as maintaining a Harley Street practice, he was also a visiting university professor. Iain and I travelled together for twelve years. One Good Friday in St Andrew's he heard the audible voice of God. He believed he had been told to give up his neurosurgery and travel with me. This part-time commitment soon became full-time. In his professional life Iain performed numerous delicate and life saving operations in which he used his scientific experience and surgeon's skills to bring healing to many people. Before he ever cut with his scalpel, he spent a few moments in silent prayer acknowledging the Lord to be the source of all healing. Yet, with equal commitment, he laid his hands on the sick and prayed for healing in the name of Jesus Christ.

For both of us our tour of Wales in 1985 was to become a turning point. During our stay we met a number of church leaders in preparation for subsequent visits by our teams. At one location we had a day off together, but agreed to minister at a small meeting in the church that evening. A lady came for prayer whose jaw was locked. Before prayer Iain described her medical condition to me. As he prayed the Holy Spirit came powerfully upon the lady and spontaneously her jaw started to move, first in an upward and then in a sideways direction. Within twenty minutes, according to Iain, she was completely healed. Hodder and Stoughton had commissioned him to write a book on healing, and he noted this incident in his diary as an example for later use. However, our trip was marred by Iain's health; he was troubled by stomach pain. I prayed with him regularly, but he did not seem to experience any alleviation of his discomfort. Later that year we went to New Zealand together with a team. Again he was not well, and on our return it was diagnosed that he had an inoperable cancer.

Iain was thirty-five years older than I, and over the years we had developed a deep relationship. Living next door, we would often be together, and as we prayed he always told me that he believed that the Lord would heal him. However, his condition gradually deteriorated, and it was through great suffering that he finally went to be with the Jesus he loved. Jesus heals, yet there will always be the mystery of suffering; understanding and help can be discovered as we invite the crucified Jesus to be with us in our suffering.

Chapter 7

SUFFERING

Our team had been invited to Bath to lead a weekend for Walcot Parish Church. During the Saturday conference Michael, a young man in his thirties, asked if I would talk with him privately. He wanted prayer that God would give him more faith. His story was not untypical; it concerned his son. As he started to relate the facts about the child, I asked his wife to join us.

Four years previously their son had been born, and within a few days he was diagnosed as being so severely handicapped that he would never walk or communicate in normal ways. The consultant's words brought feelings of anger and frustration. Whilst still in shock, they and others started to pray. They did not know what to ask for, and simply prayed that the Lord would give them strength and help their child develop in the best possible way. Unfortunately the situation was to become even more fraught. A group of praying and sincere Christians felt that God had spoken to them to the effect that, through a miracle, God would make their son well. This apparent revelation was supposedly confirmed by Scriptures. A member of the group even had a dream in which the boy was seen running through a field.

Michael and Elizabeth had never given up hope that God would intervene and these revelations seemed to confirm their deepest desires. However, the months turned into years and there was no obvious change in their son. They started to develop deep guilt feelings, believing that it was their lack of faith which prevented God working the miracle.

As their story unfolded I felt great compassion for them. It was difficult enough having to parent a child with such disability without the additional weight of false guilt. Elizabeth, an attractive young woman, gave the appearance of being tightly bound by invisible chains.

I suggested to them that 'life isn't fair'. For reasons which we can never fully understand, some people are born with mental and physical deformities. This is a mystery and certainly not a punishment from God. I suggested that the answer to their situation lay not in a miracle, but in the cross. As we talked I believed that the Holy Spirit had shown me the truth of the situation. Sympathetic and well-meaning people had made their 'desire' God's 'intention'. With as much sensitivity as I could muster, I said that God was not going to make their son well in this life, but through the power of the cross would give all the help that was needed.

These words, instead of devastating them, released a load which they had carried daily for four years. In prayer I took the cross of Jesus and, through its power, broke the false guilt which had bound and tormented them. Elizabeth sobbed deeply as the Holy Spirit ministered to the many hurts which the situation had inflicted upon her.

Later I suggested that, in their imagination, they accompany me to the cross where they could receive their son as a gift from God. This act finally broke the cycle of despair, and they were both filled with great joy and relief. To say that from then on they lived happily ever after would be a gross distortion of the facts. Every morning of their lives they will have to care for a son who is more dependent upon them than a tiny baby.

It can be equally traumatic for adults to accept their own disabilities. St Andrew's Church, Madras was, before it joined the Church of South India, a missionary church of the Scottish Presbyterian tradition. Today it is pastored by David Singh and his wife, Nalini. David invited us to the church to lead a week of evening meetings on the theme of 'God in Action'.

I was looking forward immensely to being with him as we had met two years previously at a Nagpur conference at which I was a speaker.

David had gone to Nagpur in a depressed state. Since childhood he had suffered from acute asthmatic attacks which had left him weak and frail. He confided that the demands of a large church were proving too much. Some weeks he only had two days free of breathing difficulties. We prayed together.

Before we left Nagpur he told me that waves of power had flowed through his body and his breathing had returned to normal. This situation had continued over the next two years. His renewed health, and greater confidence in the Holy Spirit, had started to transform the fellowship of the church. A number of the congregation had received healing and fringe people had come to a living faith in Jesus. Subsequently, when we arrived, the expectancy in the packed church was very high.

As I rose to speak on the first evening I was particularly conscious of a young woman in her early twenties; she was seated four rows from the front. All I could see was her head and shoulders. She was pretty, with striking facial features and black wavy hair. During my talk she seemed to hang on every word, straining forward as if she was frightened of missing something. When I had concluded I invited the Holy Spirit to minister and people started to come to the front for prayer. I was supervising this when I saw her stand up. I was initially surprised.

The young woman swung into the aisle on two crutches. She apparently had little use of her legs, and as she came to where I was standing I noticed that her back was deformed. I asked her what she would like me to pray for. She replied that she believed God would heal her physical condition that evening. Before proceeding further, I suggested that we sit and she tell me why she believed God would heal her.

Some years previously she had received Jesus as her Lord and Saviour. As she read the stories of Jesus in the Gospels,

she noticed that He healed people who had conditions such
as hers. She and her friends had regularly prayed about her
condition and had received firm promises that she would be
healed. As she was expanding on this I sensed the Holy Spirit
telling me something which I knew was going to be difficult
to say.

I told her I also believed that Jesus could heal people who
had been damaged at birth. I cited an instance. We had been
with a team in Holland where one of our young men had
prayed with a boy whose arm and hand had been deformed
at birth. Whilst he and the boy's mother prayed with him the
limb returned to normal. However, I went on to say that I
did not have the faith to believe that God was going to heal
her. With that she burst into tears and, taking her crutches,
immediately left the meeting. I felt devastated.

Later in the week she returned and sought me out. As she
approached I felt embarrassed and could not think of anything
to say. However, I need not have worried. She smiled and
thanked me. What I had said had been the most liberating
words she had heard since receiving Christ. She asked me to
take her in prayer to the cross, where she wanted to stand
with Jesus and accept her condition as being allowed by Him.
Her joy that evening was overwhelming; yet she still has a
long journey to travel, and the cross will not become any
lighter with the passing of the years.

As this book has illustrated, I believe in the healing power
of Jesus which radiates from the cross. It would seem to me
that Jesus recognised disease as a result of evil, and He was
convinced that His Father wanted men to be whole and
healthy. For this reason we have been involved, as a church,
in the healing ministry for twenty years. During this time we
have ministered to hundreds of people whose physical
symptoms have been healed in response to prayer in the name
of Jesus. However, there have been others whose physical
conditions have not responded and have consequently led to
a life of suffering, or known premature death.

I loved Hugh; he was one of the most sensitive men I have

ever met. In our worship team he played the cello. Even as I write I can still hear the deep haunting notes with which he lifted our hearts in worship. His wife Liz, played the guitar and together they often led the worship in one of our travelling teams.

We were discussing a service in which we were both to be involved when Hugh told me that he seemed to be losing his confidence. It appeared that periodically his memory would fade and for a moment he would not know what he was playing. Jokingly I suggested that it was a sign of premature old age. Unfortunately it continued and a scan revealed an inoperable brain tumour. We were devastated. God, of course, would heal. Hugh and Elizabeth had only been married for a short time. He was so young and had everything to live for. We prayed, and prayed some more, but the condition deteriorated.

Hugh and I talked much together. He was full of questions. How should he respond to the 'words' he had received from faithful and caring people to the effect that God was going to heal him? Was it his lack of faith that was holding back the healing power? Having been anointed with oil in the name of Jesus, should he be claiming the healing, or walking in faith believing that he was healed, as some suggested? Did I think there was some hidden sin in his life, that he was not conscious of, that was blocking the healing power?

Just before Hugh was admitted to the Michael Sobell Hospice at Northwood, we had an afternoon together. I remember Hugh lying on his bed, resting, as I sat in a chair nearby. I sensed that Hugh had accepted the truth. He was going to die. In fact, I do not think he ever thought he would be healed. I reminded him that here was only one place where he could find meaning for the journey ahead. Jesus had plummeted to the depths of physical suffering. This meant that, moment by moment, He would identify with each stage through which Hugh would pass. We talked at length of what lay beyond the cross. Hugh firmly believed that, because Jesus had been raised from the dead, he also would be raised to be with Him for ever.

The time we spent together at the cross transformed Hugh. Although, outwardly, he took a skeletal form, inwardly a most remarkable transformation happened. At times he glowed with the presence of God.

However, it would be wrong in any way to minimise the depth of his sufferings. Although the hospice medical staff were specialists in controlling pain, Hugh still at times plummeted to the depths of agony and despair. Yet he would want me to say that, because he believed that Jesus understood, he was able to draw on powerful resources.

We as Christians do not have answers for those who ask the question, 'Why, if there is a loving God, does He allow good people like Hugh to undergo such sufferings?' We also find the meaning of suffering an unfathomable question. However, in the blackest night and in the deepest pit, we see an inextinguishable light in the form of a cross. This alone is not an explanation, but rather a source of understanding and hope.

One Sunday morning I met Prue, a member of our staff, coming into St Andrew's. She was weeping. Prue had lived in Zimbabwe and had just heard that her dear friend, Gaynor Hill, had been brutally murdered. The unfolding story became international news.

In 1980 Gaynor and her husband, Robert, were with sixteen other Christians who left the security of Harare to establish two centres for reconciliation in Matabeleland in south-western Zimbabwe. These were based on farms called 'New Olive' and 'New Adam'. This area was frequented by dissidents who supported the ZAPU party of Mr Joshua Nkomo, and after independence still opposed the government of Robert Mugabe. The rebels had support in the area from the Ndebele peasants who were experiencing extreme poverty because of drought conditions, and they were becoming viciously anti-white.

Some twenty white farmers had been killed in the area and others had formed a group which they called 'Reaction Sticks'.

These were heavily armed militia units who responded to violence and tracked down active dissident units. Gary Keightley, leader of the community, was invited to join this organisation. He declined, saying that 'As Christians we do not believe we should seek special protection. We put our trust in the Lord.'

The communities had been robbed by rebels on more than one occasion, and as a result the team had organised a twenty-four-hour prayer chain. This meant that at all times, both day and night, a community member was praying in their chapel for God's presence and protection.

What happened on the night of Wednesday 25th November 1987 was horrendous. Prime Minister Mugabe called it 'unbridled savagery'. The president of the Farmers' Union said, 'It's quite barbaric. This is the worst, most terrible massacre we have ever seen, including the war years.' The facts, as they emerged, were these.

A dissident leader known as Gayiguso arrived at the farms with twenty dissidents. They tied up the Christians who were then axed and clubbed, one by one. Esselet Dube, an African domestic worker, was forced to watch this being done. She said, 'There were no screams, no crying, nothing but prayers as each one said farewell to me. They were then ordered at gun point into a room and hacked and beaten to death. The terrorists tossed each body outside to make room for the next. The remaining victims stood waiting to die, surrounded by the mutilated bodies of their friends and relatives.' Dube vomited as she watched her employer, Gaynor Hill, being killed.

The world media reflected the bewilderment and angry reactions of the people of Zimbabwe. Why, they demanded, would the Christian God of love allow innocent children and devout parents to be hacked to death by such evil people? Again we have no answer, except to say that the question was not a problem for the community members. They went prayerfully to their death. As disciples of Jesus they knew that it was always conceivable that the cross Jesus called them to

carry could end in a brutal death. In God's providence He
may use such tragedy for a greater purpose.

Watching the Sisters of Mercy lifting dying children from
the gutters of Calcutta, we are able to glimpse something of
the goodness to which man can attain. In stark contrast, the
atrocity on the farms of Matabeleland reveals the hidden
depths of evil to which man can sink. It may be that the
Almighty and All Powerful God allows such butcherings of
His children in order that the world may be shaken into seeing
its own heart and its need of forgiveness through His Son
Jesus.

For men living without God, suffering and death can be
viewed as the ultimate defeat. The Apostle Paul notes that
grief is a common experience of all who face loss caused by
bereavement. The grief of the unbeliever is without hope. For
them, life is like a candle. On average it lasts seven decades
and then it is snuffed out, never to be rekindled. If that is
man's perspective on life, then death is an absolute beyond
which there is no hope. However, Christian belief is radically
different.

The disciple of Jesus Christ acknowledges the ever-presence
of death. Of his final event in his life he is not afraid.
Fundamental to his belief is the fact that Jesus died and rose
again; so, he believes, will it be for those who die believing
in Jesus. God will raise them from the dead. The Christian
grieves with all men, but his grief has a hope. It is of
resurrection, being with Jesus, and a re-uniting with all those
who died as Christians. Gaynor Hill and her community died
in this faith.

Reflecting on the enigma of suffering and its apparent
unfairness the Apostle Paul writes, 'And we know that in all
things God works for the good of those who love him, who
have been called according to his purpose.' And again, 'For
I am convinced that neither death nor life, neither angels nor
demons, neither the present nor the future, nor any powers,
neither height nor depth, nor anything else in all creation,
will be able to separate us from the love of God that is in Christ

Jesus our Lord' (Romans 8:28, 38–39).

Often the most innocent suffer because they are unable to justify themselves and have to suffer misunderstanding in silence. This is what happened to Jesus. During the events leading up to His death, government and religious authorities alike tried to make Jesus deny His enemies' accusations, but He refused to do so. Even on the cross He would not be drawn into justifying Himself. He suffered in silence.

We were leading a meeting at a large church when, at the ministry time, a girl in her late teens approached me. She initiated the conversation by asking if I would believe what she had to say. Having just met, I said I had no reason not to, and encouraged her to share her situation. She had arrived in the city to work, and had gone to the church on the recommendation of friends. She had only been a Christian for a year, and was delighted when one of the elders and his wife invited her to lodge with them. After a few months he seduced her, and she became frightened as she did not know how to extract herself from the situation.

Eventually she could not deal with her guilt feelings and went to the pastor of the church to confess and put her life right again with God. Subsequently he confronted the elder concerned, who was indignant and denied any sexual involvement with the girl. As often happens in such situations, the details were leaked and soon became a scandal in the church. The accused's wife was devastated by the rumours, as was his family. However, the husband maintained his innocence and the girl felt that, for his family's sake, she would tell the pastor that she had imagined the whole incident. Because the church was large and the elder was well-known, she was made to deny publicly that he had had any sexual involvement with her. As the story unfolded her eyes filled with tears and, looking straight at me, she said that she had originally told the truth. The elder had seduced her.

I believed her story. She felt hurt and humiliated, and wanted the church to know she was not the type of person that many thought she was. I sought to dissuade her from raising the situation again, especially as the leader concerned adamantly denied her accusation. However, it was at the cross that I helped her to discover the real situation. Here I pointed to Jesus, the innocent, who did not justify Himself before men but accepted the misunderstandings and trusted Himself to His Heavenly Father. As we prayed I asked her to picture all those who had falsely accused her, and in Jesus' name to forgive them. The Holy Spirit came upon her powerfully and she rested in His presence. Outwardly the situation remained unchanged; she still had to live with people's misunderstanding of her, yet inwardly peace and joy returned.

The cross only has power because Jesus was perfectly obedient to His Father. In the Garden of Gethsemane, when confronted with the reality of the cross, He asked His Father if it were possible for Him to accomplish His will any other way. However, He ends with the words of absolute submission, 'not my will, but yours be done' (Luke 22:42).

I met Ruth when she requested prayer after one of our meetings. It was a familiar story. Her husband, a lively and career orientated executive, had been moved by his firm to suburbia within commuting distance from London. He left the house at seven and returned in the evening between seven and ten. Consequently the young children's opportunity for seeing him was at the weekend when, often as not, he was either catching up on office work or out playing golf.

After seven years of marriage Ruth felt lonely and tied to the house and young family. Her husband had little time to communicate and when he did he was not interested in how she was feeling. Inevitably, Ruth met a man in her village who was kind and listened sympathetically to her problems. Within a few months she was emotionally attached to him.

Ruth was confused. Realising that her marriage had died, she prayed that God would do something to change the situation. Within a few weeks the new man came into her life. Consequently she had convinced herself that he was God's answer to her prayers. As we talked together I read the Scriptures which outlined God's intention for marriage. It was to be a life-long commitment. To protect this relationship, God had placed it within certain boundaries. He forbade adultery because it would hurt and damage the marriage, and all concerned.

Ruth listened intently. She understood the logic of what I was saying but felt that she was so emotionally involved that it would be impossible to relinquish the relationship. In fact, initially she did not want to. She felt that finally she was living again and becoming the person God created her to be.

I drew her attention to the cross where Jesus had aligned Himself with His Father's will. In her situation the Father's will was that she recommit herself to her husband. This involved forgiving him and confessing and renouncing the wrong emotional relationship she had developed. This was not an easy decision but, after much discussion, Ruth realised that it was the only one possible as a disciple of Jesus. As she responded to Jesus in prayer, I placed the cross between her and the other man, and broke the emotional ties. Again, it was not a 'happy ever after' ending.

Now, after ten years, her marriage is no different. Her husband's business has taken over completely. He still plays golf at the weekends, and cannot believe that there is any problem in their relationship. When occasionally she has broached the subject, he has referred to the incredible provision he has made for her and the family. It would be much easier to opt out of the relationship but Ruth knows that it is not God's will for her to do so.

In the providence of God, suffering has an integral part to play in the character development of a disciple of Jesus. The Apostle Paul records an experience he and Titus had in the province of Asia. He writes of the great pressure, far beyond their ability to endure, so that they despaired even of life. However, he accepted the suffering in a positive way. He believed that the experience enabled them to rely on God who, if the worst did happen, would raise them from the dead. Yet he viewed the suffering in a still wider context. In it he had received God's comfort in order that he could comfort others with the comfort he had received. Experiences of the cross are to radiate outwards from the disciple in order that he or she might serve others in the name of Jesus.

Chapter 8

CALLED TO SERVE

In my first job I was given responsibility for the young people. Initially this was not terribly onerous as only about half a dozen teenagers were attached to the church, of whom two attended worship. After eighteen months this group had grown to about one hundred and fifty, of whom twenty attended. They met after the evening worship service in a large room above what was once the rectory stables. With so many attending we had a problem of seating, and so I persuaded a large departmental store to give a few dozen carpet squares. With these we made an enormous multi-coloured carpet.

This group had grown so quickly because, except for visiting the pubs, there was little else for young people to do on a Sunday evening west of Plymouth! A nucleus had become Christians, but were still working out the implications of their faith at a Friday night fellowship group which Mary and I led in our house. After lunch on Sunday I would prepare what was known as 'The Rectory Room' for the evening meeting. A number from the nucleus always intended to join me, but never quite made it.

On one occasion I found that a group of boys had used the room. They left it in such disorder that it looked as if a hurricane had given a couple of blows through the door. Paper, cigarette ends, empty cans and cups half-filled with coffee littered the entire room. The group had apparently arrived via the woods and ploughed fields. Hunks of dried mud were embedded in the carpet.

I found a rubbish bin and started the job of collecting the debris. As I worked I became progressively more angry. Addressing imaginary church authorities, I told them it was not fair that I, as leader, should also have to be caretaker. My fury reached a crescendo when, on my knees, I applied an ancient vacuum cleaner which blew out more dust than it sucked in. In vain I tried to break up and remove the mud. Sitting back on my haunches, with perspiration soaking my shirt, I then told God that it was just not good enough. I had been ordained into the Anglican ministry in order to preach the Gospel, not to clean up young people's rubbish. At that moment the events surrounding Jesus' cross came into my mind. With this general impression I remembered His words to His disciples when He told them that He ' . . . did not come to be served, but to serve, and to give his life as a ransom for many' (Mark 10:45). I thought of Him in the upper room assuming the position of a servant, and after washing His disciples' feet, He said to them, 'I have set you an example that you should do as I have done for you. I tell you the truth, no servant is greater than his master, nor is a messenger greater than the one who sent him. Now that you know these things you will be blessed if you do them' (John 13:15–16).

Some years later I was to join the staff at St Andrew's. I was soon on the rota to lead the early morning Communion Service. On my arrival I always found the table covered in a brilliant white cloth, and the bread and wine ready for use. It never occurred to me that someone actually had to make these preparations until one particular Saturday evening. I was returning home late and found that the lights were on in the church. Thinking it may have been a break-in, I went to investigate. I found 'Mrs Mac', an elderly lady, busy cleaning the carpet and making preparations for the early morning service. She had been doing that for nearly forty years.

In a church such as ours the spotlight often falls on the two hundred lay people whom our vicar David has authorised to pray for people after our services. At other times it is on those who travel with the faith sharing teams. Such ministries also require sacrifice of time but it is those who humbly serve with 'the towel' that Jesus terms 'the greatest'.

As a leader of a team that travels to many parts of the world, I am especially aware of the unifying power of a person who serves. In response to an invitation I led a team to New Zealand to minister at various conferences and regional centres. In accepting the invitation I had requested that, wherever possible, the team stay together. This meant that, when we were not at a conference centre, we stayed in large private homes whose owners either moved in with friends or were on holiday. An itinerant ministry lasting five weeks has its own unique demands. It involves living out of a suitcase which is continually being unpacked, packed and skilfully placed with ten others in a mini-van. Long, hot journeys cramped together are relieved by meals which team members produce on a rotation basis. Sometimes, because of unforeseen circumstances, the team arrives at a venue with hardly time to freshen up before a meeting.

Whilst leading a conference we would often have to leave our accommodation early and travel to the venue. After a day of talks, seminars and leading worship, we would have a short break before a public meeting in the evening. The numbers attending our meetings might vary between one hundred and three thousand. At the conclusion we always invited the Holy Spirit to minister and this meant being available to pray with people until ten o'clock or later.

Tired and emotionally sapped, we drove home. On the way we either collected a selection of fast food from McDonald's or shared the preparation of a meal on arrival. By the time we had eaten, the kitchen and dining room were usually littered with dirty crockery and food containers.

Over coffee I always asked the team to share the day's events. They would recount both the encouraging and the disappointments. In the light of this sharing we decided on any change we needed to make the following day. This report-back seldom ended before one o'clock in the morning. As it

was so late I usually suggested that we go to bed and leave
the mess to be cleared up in the morning. The team needed
no persuading as they flopped into welcome beds.

As long as I can remember I have woken each morning
a few minutes before six o'clock. I usually make a cup of tea
before prayer. On our travels, whenever I went to make tea
in the kitchen, I found it in pristine condition. The chaos of
the night before had disappeared. The floor sparkled and the
crockery was clean and in its rightful place. This happened
regularly and, although I acknowledged it, no one took the
credit.

Arising particularly early one morning, I found George,
the eldest team member, busy mopping the kitchen floor. He
was the secret cleaner and odd job man. An example to us
of a servant spirit.

Reflecting on the team's ministry, I was conscious how
individuals had matured in their gifts of teaching, preaching,
witnessing, prophecy, healing and worship. Reading articles
on our tour which appeared in newspapers and magazines,
it would seem that many individuals and churches had been
helped to minister in the power of the Holy Spirit through
our visit. Yet without George taking the servant's role, the
oil could have dried up and we would have 'grated' along
together. This attitude is so contrary to human nature which
wants above all else to be served, and to be seen in positions
of power and authority.

The greatest act of serving is seen in Jesus' death on the
cross. During His life He gave many examples which illustrate
the cost involved in serving. On one occasion He assumed
the role of a slave and washed His disciples' dirty and dusty
feet. He showed that serving involves putting aside your own
wishes and desires in order that the needs of others can be
met. The event of the cross is the Christian's inspiration for
the serving of others. Men need their feet washed but their
greater need is for forgiveness, security, freedom from fear
and demonic affliction. They need hope in suffering and
death. Jesus served these great needs on the cross, in that He

gave His life as a ransom in order that we might be liberated from them. The cross encompasses all that Jesus meant when He spoke of 'laying down your own life for a friend'.

I had only been a Christian for a few months before moving to live with my parents in Jerusalem. On one occasion I visited the Holy Sepulchre, the supposed site of the crucifixion of Jesus. Many people were present as the Eastern churches were celebrating their Easter. One of the attractions of the festival, for tourists, was a procession which was led by young men who were training for the priesthood.

I had arrived early and climbed a wall on to the roof of a Coptic church where I had an uninterrupted view of the proceedings. As crowds gathered a fight broke out amongst the priests. They shouted and pushed each other as they fought over a large crucifix needed for the procession. Order was restored when a senior priest strode into their midst, grabbed the crucifix and handed it to a young man who had not taken part in the affray. Peace was restored; the procession, with great dignity and reverence, made its way around the building towards the Sepulchre entrance.

I so easily identified with the young men who fought for the prime position in the procession. Some years later I was studying in London and the evangelist Billy Graham was holding a series of meetings at Earl's Court. One evening his organisation had invited, as guests, those at the theological college who had come to know Christ through his ministry. Twenty of us from evangelical training colleges had responded to the invitation. Soon we found ourselves jockeying for position on the platform. There was a vast crowd at Earl's Court that night as Cliff Richard, then a young Christian, was going to give his testimony.

With us on the platform were a number of prominent Christian leaders, together with others like myself who would have liked to be prominent. With skill and a certain amount of daring, I managed to get a seat just behind Billy, Cliff and a retired bishop. I was hoping that at least someone in authority would take note of my presence and position for a

future occasion! I still had to learn that such attitudes were
the exact opposite to all that Jesus taught about leadership
in the light of the cross. His leaders are those who serve.
Meeting such servants is an awe-inspiring experience because
in them we meet Christ.

On one occasion I took a team to Nairobi to lead a
conference sponsored by a group called Anglican Renewal,
Kenya. We were based on St Stephen's Church, which played
host to the leaders who came from various parts of Kenya.
The opening of the conference was attended by church
dignitaries, including the Archbishop. Yet amongst all the
people we were to meet subsequently, there was one man who
stood head and shoulders above the rest. Gilbert Amimo was
pastor of a three-thousand-member church. He was a man
who radiated humility. On the big occasions he always
positioned himself on the periphery of the dignitaries. When
discussing the day's programme with our team, he sought all
the time to promote others and take the serving role himself.
His sole object was to seek the mind of Christ, irrespective
of what it cost him personally. He suffered much as he led
his church into renewal and faced up to the consequences.

Such attitudes of humility can be taken for weakness, but
as we observe the ministry of Jesus and others who have
followed Him in the servant role we see that this is not so.
Gilbert was indeed a leader with a 'terrier like' tenacity when
it came to doing what he felt the Lord was saying to him.
As strange as it may seem, this way of servanthood inspires
others to follow in the same way.

Whilst ministering in Calcutta I often stayed at the Baptist
hostel, which is situated in the same road as one of Mother
Teresa's homes for the destitute. I visited one of these homes
one morning and was treated to a most unusual experience.
It was washing time for the babies who had come to the hostel
from various sources. A number had been left at the Convent
door, wrapped in newspapers. The Sisters had found others
abandoned on the streets, or thrust into their hands by
mothers who could no longer cope. They were all

undernourished, and the majority had sores and scabs on many parts of their bodies.

The Sisters had formed a conveyor belt using a number of tables, trestles and a large bed. The first Sister put the baby in a soapy tub of warm water. She handed it on to the second who immersed it in a tub of clear water. The next towelled the baby dry before handing it on to the masseuse who rubbed oil into its body. Another Sister put the nappy on, whilst the final one applied ointment and dressings before placing the baby on the large bed. When this process was completed, there were almost two dozen babies gurgling and wriggling together.

At various times I have spoken with the Sisters and sought to discover what motivated them. The answer I initially expected was 'Christ'. Indirectly it was, but many had encountered Him first through the life of their founder, Mother Teresa. It was as they watched her serving the poor that they met Christ and wanted to live the same way of life.

Christ's call to serve is not just seeking to meet the physical and spiritual needs of others; it also involves prayer. This is an area in which Jesus served His disciples. He told Peter that a personal crisis lay ahead of him and the team, but He had prayed for them that their faith would not fail. On other occasions He prays that His Father would protect His followers from the evil one.

In the early seventies I had a book published entitled *Springtime in the Church*. An elderly member of our congregation told me that she was delighted to hear about my book entitled 'Spring Cleaning the Church'. Because of impaired hearing, she had mistaken the book's title; yet in other respects she was spiritually in tune with all that was happening in our fellowship which she served through prayer. Sometimes she would sidle up to me and, in her quiet, unassuming way, ask a pertinent question regarding a church weekend we had been leading. It would transpire that she found herself praying for us in a particular way, and wondered whether what she sensed was in fact the situation. In many instances, it was.

If the mark of the cross in a believer's life is seen in his

willingness to serve, so it should be the mark of the church
to which he belongs. Fifteen years ago I founded the Faith
Sharing Ministry based on St Andrew's Church. This was
in response to what I believed to have been a call of God.
Our church leadership unanimously agreed to set me aside
for this purpose, and to review the ministry after a year. Little
did we know what it was going to cost.

The idea I had was to invite together thirty members of
our congregation to form the nucleus team. I foresaw that,
after a year's experience, they in turn would sub-divide into
many teams. Initially it was exciting as the team met and
started to travel. Reports of what God had done through them
encouraged the church. However, rumblings soon started.
Some asked why they had not been included in the teams.
Others pointed to the fact that many of the key leaders were
regularly away, and wondered why they were not involved
in the less romantic jobs of teaching in the Sunday School
or helping in the youth work. On occasions an outreach to
a nearby town meant that two hundred people were absent
from the Sunday worship. Those left behind felt slightly
'second class'. Gradually the whole church was faced with
the cost of such a ministry, as up to six teams latterly have
been away at any given weekend. However, the cross principle
is to sacrifice and give. At the church at Antioch they gave
away their best leaders in order that the church might grow.
Jesus taught that it is by giving that we receive more of His
blessing.

I realised that this ministry could only grow if I gave away
people. I gathered around me those who were gifted in
leadership, in the teaching and prophetic ministry, together
with those anointed to lead in worship, and to heal the sick.
Working closely together, a special bond of love and
commitment develops. My natural tendency was to keep those
people bound to myself. However, I knew that unless I was
prepared to release them, the work which God was doing
would be hampered.

On one occasion I assembled a team of ten for ministry

which would mean travelling together for a month. Included were Richard and Prue Bedwell. I had first met them eight years previously when the London Bible College asked me if I would take them on a Faith Sharing team. Richard had been made redundant in the take-over of a business which his father had founded. Instead of accepting a new job offer, he decided to retire and with Prue study at a Bible college before seeking full-time Christian employment.

The outreach was based on St Peter's, Hextable over an Easter period. Early each morning the team met in the church to pray. On the third morning, whilst we were waiting on the Lord, I started to think of Richard and Prue. Suddenly the Lord said to me, 'Invite them to join the staff.' Since I had no authority to do this I conveyed my thoughts to David. On our return he met them and invited them on to our staff as counsellors. They subsequently were to travel with me, including a trip around the world.

Our team for this particular ministry was meeting to pray and I had booked the flights. David had been away in America and when he returned he told me that he did not think it right that Richard and Prue should accompany me on my next tour to New Zealand, since I was also taking our lady deacon from the staff. This was difficult. Besides being gifted teachers and counsellors, Richard is an excellent administrator and I felt I needed him on such an undertaking so far from home. On my weekly retreat I spent time talking it over with the Lord. As I prayed it seemed to me that He was telling me to 'give them away'. He now wanted them to travel with David and Mary. With a certain amount of sadness, I offered them to the Lord.

Subsequently they have not travelled at all with me, but for the last four years have supported David and Mary in their ministries to America, Africa, Australia and Canada and many parts of England.

Unfortunately, for us to travel this way, our families have also to give us away and this can be painful for each member. One summer holiday when we were in France our daughter,

Noonie, started reminiscing on certain events of the previous
fifteen years. Ever since she could remember I had been
travelling, and she shared how rejected she had felt at times
by my absence. She reminded me that each January on her
birthday, for a number of years, I had been abroad. I told
her that in the southern hemisphere this is the time when
conferences and conventions are held, and that I had felt it
right to accept invitations from those places. She went on to
tell me that, even when I returned, she found it difficult as
I was tired and unable initially to give her the time and
attention she wanted.

I asked her if she wished I had a settled job and been home
regularly. She replied that she did not. She saw our separation
as part of the cost our family paid being able to give away
the Gospel. Two years after this conversation she was also
travelling with our team. She accompanied me on a trip to
Africa and was able to experience at first hand the power of
the Gospel in a different culture.

During this conversation Mary also recalled the numerous
parties, social events, dinners and church celebrations that
she had attended, alone. She said that this was sometimes
difficult for her, but she accepted it as part of the cost of giving
away the Gospel.

Some years ago David and I started a monthly Celebration
service. We chose the third Saturday of the month and invited
any who would care to come and join us. The format was
simple: we commenced with praise, followed by testimonies,
worship, preaching and ministry in the power of the Holy
Spirit. On the first occasion about thirty attended. We never
advertised the meeting but, as the months passed, the numbers
grew. It was then that we decided to have not just an evening,
but a whole day. On the Saturday morning David started a
series of seven seminars based on various aspects of ministering
in the power of the Holy Spirit. One of our non-stipendiary
clergy, Bob Maynard, started afternoon workshops and others
volunteered to keep the kitchen going with drinks of tea and
coffee. Latterly numbers for the morning were around five

hundred and, by the evening, eight hundred.

One staff meeting we discussed the Celebration Day in great detail. It was obvious that the gathering had outgrown our facilities, and was drawing people from the Greater London area and beyond. As we talked it became apparent that we should close it down and disperse the people to other centres. This was a difficult decision. Success in Christian circles is always gauged by numbers. Whenever people ask me about a meeting where I have spoken, their first question will be about its size. If twenty attended, it would be judged mediocre, whereas if as many as two hundred and fifty were present, then it would have been successful. Our meetings gave us a platform to preach and minister to hundreds of people. At any Celebration a show of hands would indicate that there were usually large numbers of new people present. The natural desire was to hold on and build for ourselves, but the way of the cross is always to give away. When David announced the decision to close the Celebration Day, a wave of sadness swept through our fellowship. We decided to invite a number of ministers in the Home Counties to host a monthly Celebration in their area. Their response was encouraging and at least twelve new centres have since been established. Jesus said that, unless a seed of wheat falls into the ground and dies, it remains alone; but if it dies, it will reproduce itself in remarkable ways. We allowed our seed to fall and die, and have experienced much joy in seeing other Celebrations grow and flourish.

We have a regular prophetic ministry operating in our church. Over a period of weeks a theme started to develop in the messages. The Lord seemed to be saying that He had given us much and He wanted us to give our church away. For me, one prophetic utterance was particularly memorable when the speaker told us that he felt that the Lord was saying, 'Get out, get out, get out'.

On every agenda of our Parochial Church Council there is the question 'What is the Holy Spirit saying to the church?' The council considered the general theme of the prophecies coupled with some practical suggestions put to them by the staff. The result was that we planted two churches in our parish. On paper and in theory this can be exciting, but when it actually happens there is a deep sense of mutual bereavement.

There were many in the sizeable foundation groups whom I had come to know and love over many years. Some I first met when they tentatively attended worship. I had seen them come to faith in Jesus and enter into the fullness of the Holy Spirit's blessing. A number were members of home groups we attended. The break, when it came, was a decisive one. We allowed them under their leadership the freedom to develop in worship and evangelism in whatever way they sensed the Lord was leading them. This move was seen to have been motivated by the Holy Spirit, as both fellowships have doubled in size, with people who have not before attended St Andrew's.

Whereas the leadership was interpreting the prophecies as they related to the congregation as a whole, individuals were also responding in costly and dynamic ways. David and Viv had been part of the fellowship at St Andrew's for many years and taken an active part in leading home groups. David worked in the City and held a senior position in the world of banking. I invited them both to be members of a team which ministered at a residential conference in Cornwall. At the end of the conference the then warden of Trelowarren Manor, John Dibbs Smith, asked David and Viv if they would consider replacing him as wardens of the small Christian community. Within a relatively short period David had resigned from the bank and moved to the community. It was because the Lord said 'Get out'.

Many of our older teenagers felt compelled to respond. Paul, a local doctor's son, was given a deep compassion for the homeless who live on the streets of London. To start with he went into the City a few nights each week and spent time talking with, and getting to know, the drop-outs. Many of them confided in him, and he sought to help practically by bringing clothes and making enquiries on their behalf with the various housing associations. His contacts grew to such an extent that he decided to go and live with them. This involved making himself a cardboard box shelter.

The Lord Jesus honoured this act of obedience. On one occasion a slightly unbalanced man took a knife to him with the express intention of cutting his throat. Paul felt it was divine intervention that protected him from a violent incident. A friend of Paul's tells the story of how one night Paul had heard a young woman in a cardboard box nearby crying with cold. He took off his woollen sweater and gave it to her. Later the same evening a man nearby was also shivering. All Paul had was a tee-shirt; he removed this and gave it. As he did so the glory of the Lord fell upon him.

Others, like Chris, committed themselves to a year working with a church in a deprived area of the country. A number of young couples left to join churches which were just starting to come alive and grow. When people adopt a serving role and are obedient to the Lord's call, their going brings not only a sense of loss but also of great joy. The dying to self in order that life may come to others is one of the great principles of the cross. Speaking of His impending crucifixion Jesus said, 'The hour has come for the Son of Man to be glorified. I tell you the truth, unless a grain of wheat falls to the ground and dies, it remains only a single seed. But if it dies, it produces many seeds' (John 12:23–24).

Chapter 9

THIRTY-NINE STEPS

One of the strange aspects of the life and ministry of Jesus is the constant and persistent rejection He received. He was born into a nation that had been prepared through prophecy for His coming, but when He started to minister in love He experienced a growing hostility which culminated in His crucifixion. His healings were opposed. After He exorcised the demonised He was called the prince of darkness. His teaching about the Kingdom of God and application of the Jewish law drew much anger and resentment, as did His attitude to their religious traditions. He was to say, quoting from Isaiah:

> These people come near to me with their mouth
>   and honour me with their lips,
>   but their hearts are far from me.
> Their worship of me
>   is made up only of rules taught by men.
>   (Isaiah 29:13)

Jesus was seeking to bring life to a religion which gave the appearance of being sincere but was actually spiritually weak and ineffective. As He challenged traditional forms of worship and theological interpretations of the Scriptures, so He experienced ever-increasing degrees of suffering. He was the 'suffering servant' of Isaiah whose suffering started in earnest immediately following His baptism. Jesus told His disciples that if this was how He was treated as He sought to bring new life to old religious structures, they were not to be surprised as they experienced similar suffering. When the life of Jesus, with its many implications concerning worship and living, is worked out in a traditional congregation, then those involved need to be constantly reflecting on, and drawing strength from, the sufferings of Jesus. They will discover that there is no spiritual power without the cross, and equally that new life follows suffering.

On a number of occasions David and I have hosted an autumn gathering for church leaders at the Swanwick Conference Centre. Recently I was teaching on the prophecies of Haggai in which he calls the Church to return to its first priority of worship. I noted from the book that a group within the Church took the message to heart whilst others responded negatively. I then caricatured the way in which some congregations react to changes which seek to make the worship of God more relevant. I began with the vicar standing at the church door and shaking hands with his congregation after another service in which a more spontaneous form of worship had taken place.

A very staid, middle-aged lady approaches him. She quickly passes by, exclaiming as she goes, 'People don't like it, Vicar'. She is followed by the choir master; he is slightly flushed and very agitated. 'Vicar,' he blurts out with ever rising emotion, 'if you have any more of those new songs, Miss Jones in the choir is going to resign and take her nephew with her.' Next the local doctor, an ex-churchwarden, asks the vicar if he could have a quiet word. 'Peter,' he begins, 'you may have noticed my wife leave the church when the guitar group started to play. She is not coming back if you continue with those terrible ditties.'

On the Wednesday Peter has an early morning telephone call. 'Hallo, Peter, it's your Bishop. I've just received a letter from Major Bonnington-Smith. He says he is writing on behalf of a large group within your church. Peter, what are you doing with the liturgy?' During the remainder of the week a number of letters are received at the vicarage, culminating with one from the church secretary on the Friday evening. She says that several members of the Parochial Church Council would like a discussion on the place of Anglican worship in our church. The following Monday there is another early morning telephone call. 'Hallo, Peter, it's your Bishop again. I had a call from Sir Humphrey late last night. Peter, he's livid. He says that you've introduced guitars, an overhead projector and strange songs into the church. I would like you to come up this afternoon and talk with me.' Such caricatures were met with much laughter. However, for many leaders present they were not just caricatures, but painfully real situations they were having to cope with. In extreme cases it can lead to a clergyman being asked to leave his church.

I was looking forward to visiting a church in the West of England. It had been featured in an Anglican publication as the fastest growing congregation in the Church of England. However, some months prior to our proposed visit Malcolm, the priest-in-charge, wrote a rather short letter saying that he was having a certain amount of trouble and, in the circumstances, thought it better that we did not go. Six months later, Mary and I were travelling west on a ministry trip, so I contacted him and asked whether we could visit. He and his wife kindly invited us for lunch. Coming off the motorway, we eventually found the church as we wound through a large, modern housing estate. As they greeted us I could clearly see strain reflected in their faces. Over lunch they unfolded a sad story.

Although their church served a population of thousands, it was still under the ultimate authority of a 'Mother' church which was ancient in years and more liberal in approach. Our curate friend had started visiting his area and inviting people to his Sunday service. He planned within the services to cater for the whole family. At the same time he started a meeting in his home where people could gather to learn about Christ and to worship Him. As people came to know Christ they started to experience His power and many exercised the gifts of the Holy Spirit, such as prophecy and speaking in tongues. Under the inspiration of the Holy Spirit, the congregation grew considerably. It became the talking point of the area; many new families attended out of curiosity and later were wonderfully converted to Jesus.

However, just prior to our visit the vicar at the parish church had forbidden him to preach or minister in the daughter church any more. Our friend was absolutely flabbergasted; in effect he was given the sack. He visited the Bishop and explained in detail what was happening in his church and how his vicar had forbidden him to minister any more. The Bishop made two conflicting decisions. Firstly he said he must stay on and then, within a few weeks, unable to remedy the situation, asked our friend to leave. His licence to minister was revoked and a month's notice given to leave the house. He and his wife were truly broken; they believed that, in the best interests of the church, it was better that they did not contest the decision in any way, but rather accept it as a cross to be borne. Through the experience our friend developed a duodenal ulcer, for which he was undergoing medical treatment. Before we left Mary and I prayed over them, not only for God's guidance in the situation, but also for physical healing.

During periods of suffering there is always the hope of a resurrection. This was subsequently true for Malcolm and his wife. He was offered a senior position in charge of a town centre church. He also told us that his ulcer had been completely healed. The church was devastated by his treatment but, although young, was mature enough to draw together and commit themselves to the new man when he eventually arrived.

When hearing of such situations, people often ask me why such changes need to be inflicted upon a religious tradition which has served the English people for nearly four hundred years. Maybe the answer is discovered in the question, 'What is the Church, and for what purpose does it exist?'

Our traditional use of the word 'church' belies its real

meaning. When the majority of people speak of a church they are referring to the building which has been a prominent landmark in their town or village for maybe hundreds of years. Whereas when the New Testament writers refer to 'church' they are meaning a group of people who have been gathered together by God the Father, in order that they might worship His Son Jesus Christ, in the power of the Holy Spirit.

The Church exists primarily to worship Jesus as Lord, and secondly to make Him known to the community in which it is situated. Perhaps ninety-five per cent of our nation does not attend a place of worship. One of the main reasons for this is that they find what we do completely irrelevant to their daily lives. This is in sharp contrast to the Church depicted in the New Testament which, although often beset with problems, was throbbing with a spiritual vitality and power which drew people to God and transformed lives.

During the last fifteen years our teams have ministered in hundreds of churches, which have been mainly Anglican. The situations where we have been invited have been those where the leader has been conscious of the spiritual deadness and irrelevance of many of the forms of worship and church activity, and longs for God to act. Usually he has surrounded himself with a group who meet regularly to worship, pray and study the Scriptures. As they meet and fellowship in this way the Holy Spirit starts to work in a new way with them. There is a desire to share this life with the wider congregation, and they invite us to come as a catalyst which will facilitate this to happen.

The following quotation is part of a letter from the vicar of a church in Lincolnshire to which one of our leaders took a team.

We are still taking in all the events of the weekend, which have given us so much encouragement. Last night sixteen people (including Alison and myself) sat in the lounge here to share their experiences, and they were bubbling with joy. They included both churchwardens, the treasurer, and the

P.C.C. secretary, so there is a wonderful unity amongst the church officers. When we worshipped, the Holy Spirit once again came in power; we were given a prophecy, several words of knowledge, and one person spoke in tongues for the first time. Debbie's experience was the most interesting; she had a tremendous sense of power in her hands, which were tingling – but she did not know what she was meant to be doing with them. No answer came at first so I asked if anyone would like prayer for healing. One person responded, but when Debbie tried to get to her, she couldn't move. Alison's hands were now tingling as well, so we linked her and Debbie and waited. Debbie then had a mental picture of someone else in the room, and found she could easily walk over to her. She and Alison prayed and ministered together, and the Lord did a work of inner healing and release. I noticed that He was using two people who had received inner healing themselves during the weekend; so we are greatly encouraged and uplifted.

When the Holy Spirit comes in power two major events occur. Firstly, the believers are anointed and often overwhelmed by His presence, and secondly, unbelievers turn in repentance to Jesus. Both of these 'happenings' are a challenge and a threat to the status quo. Jesus said that the old wineskin could not contain new wine: they had either to soften and change, or burst. This is the most crucial problem facing the Church today. For the church leader this is inevitably the beginning of a conflict. He has to decide whether he is going to take up his cross and identify himself with Christ and His ministry, or compromise. To understand the cause of the conflict and suffering experienced by such leaders, we need to consider the distinct kinds of situations in which the Church of England finds itself today. Each of the following descriptions is slightly caricatured. In the rural areas the Church is small and struggling, with sometimes up to six small parishes being ministered to by one man. It is inclined to be traditional and reactionary towards any change. The story of the churchwarden from such a situation may not be far from the truth. A visiting Bishop congratulated him on his thirty-five years' service to the church, and reminisced on the fact that he must have seen some changes. He replied that he had, and opposed every one. I once met such a man in rural Dorset who could remember the time when, if the parson told the Lord of the Manor that he was not in church on Sunday, then he was not paid his wages.

Our first visit to a village church took me by surprise. Prior to the team's arrival for a week of faith sharing, I attended the main service at a village church to which we had been invited. I arrived early and sat on the back row and watched the morning congregation assemble. First to arrive were the elderly. Then there were some obviously middle-class people, married couples, and couples represented by the wife. The men were either in business or one of the professions, and commuted the ten miles to the major town.

A group of children suddenly appeared. The wardens and others in authority kept telling them not to talk and to tiptoe to their pew, which was just below the pulpit.

With the tolling of the bells, a vice-admiral and other military persons arrived with their wives. Approaching two minutes to eleven, his Lordship walked in with his wife and a number of country people. This was the cue for the choir to leave the vestry and process the seventy yards to their stalls.

Such a pyramidal structure has ancient origins; it goes back to the times when the Lord of the Manor and the rector controlled the lives of all the people in their parishes. From this pinnacle of power the pecking order within the parish was established. Today, with few exceptions, absolute power has gone but an invisible power structure still operates in a variety of ways.

During a week in this parish our team shared the Gospel in homes, on the street, and wherever people met. Every evening in the home meetings, invited guests committed their lives to Christ. Many Christians were filled with the Holy Spirit and spoke in tongues. One of the highlights for me was the final Sunday morning. I had spoken on the cross and invited people forward to receive Christ.

From the back of the church a tall, young Navy officer marched to the front and stood to attention. I asked him what he would like me to pray for. He replied, 'To receive Christ.' I felt that the best way for him to do this would be to answer the questions we ask candidates at baptism. So, whilst he still stood to attention, I asked him the threefold questions: Do you turn to Christ? Do you repent of your sins? Do you renounce the Devil and all his works? To all these he replied with a firm 'yes'. He had hardly said the final 'yes' when the Holy Spirit came on him in such power that he crumpled to the ground.

Amongst many in that church and village there was a tremendous rejoicing. However, others were concerned. A few weeks later the Lord of the Manor called on the vicar to have a discreet word. Graciously he told him that he and his family and a few close friends were, for the foreseeable future, going to another church led by an excellent priest who maintained all the good Anglican traditions. Such a move in a small community had a devastating effect and caused much pain in the vicarage. Hurtful rumours started to spread.

The inner city is different again. This is often a 'ghetto' situation. Those who attend worship have found safety and security within the small congregation. For many, their childhood environment has been demolished and their family homes replaced by high-rise flats. Often neighbours and friends have moved out, finding employment in other areas, and minority groups have moved in. The only constant feature in their changing world is the church with its old liturgy and worship.

Here there is also a power structure. Often it is through families. Father may be churchwarden, mother the organist, and daughter the fourth member of the choir. Their Uncle Joe may be treasurer, and his wife Eileen look after the free-will offering envelopes. If it is not through families, it is through strong individuals who have survived the redevelopment of the area. In contrast, in one inner city church we visited, none of the leaders lived closer than three miles from the parish. They had all bettered themselves and moved out, but liked returning once a week to what they had always known.

I well remember leading a team to such a church for a week of meetings. Even after ten years I can still recall vividly the first Sunday evening. It was November. The building could seat eight hundred comfortably but that night there were thirty present, excluding ourselves. Most of the congregation were dressed in duffle coats, scarves and gloves. As it was a special guest evening the heating had been on for four hours, but I doubt if it had even warmed the pipes. A number of prominent personalities insisted the opening meeting be in the church. The clergy were expected to robe and process with the two choir members. One of the highlights of the evening was a burst water pipe, high in the ceiling, which sent down torrents of water which froze in patterns on the wall. Needless to say, the organist played on.

During our week of mission no new people came to the home meetings and there were no conversions. However, a number of Christians were filled with the Holy Spirit and joined the vicar and his wife in their longing for change. They were soon confronted by those who found change of any description difficult.

Suburbia has been our home for twenty years. In such areas congregations are mainly middle-class, well-educated and informed. The majority of men are in managerial positions and used to taking authority and making decisions. Here the power structure is more difficult to ascertain as it is divided between the managerial and theological. The former see the church's life in terms of a four-year plan and are eager to know in detail where the church is going; the latter are concerned with theological orthodoxy as defined by either the Anglo-Catholic or Evangelical wing of the Church.

Jesus called the Holy Spirit the Counsellor (John 14:16). The greek word is παραλητος and means literally 'the One who is called alongside.' The Holy Spirit, although He is Lord and God, does not seem to come except by invitation. He never forces himself upon a person but respects the individual's freedom of choice.

When I am at home during the summer months, one of my joys is choosing a road in our parish and visiting door to door. People's responses are interesting and varied. There are those who see you coming and do not think that you have seen them, so they disappear to the back of the house and ignore the door bell when it is rung. Others see you approaching and, for politeness's sake, open the door and chat to you on the doorstep. Finally, there are the people who genuinely want to see you, and welcome you into their homes and families, being delighted to share their hospitality with you.

Today, some of our churches do not give the Holy Spirit a thought from one year to the next. He is the 'it' who is basically ignored or, because of fear, marginalised and avoided. However, there is an increasing number of churches of all denominations who are seeking to restore Him to His rightful place in the midst of God's people. They are calling upon Him to come and act amongst them in the name of Jesus. He is being honoured again. In the church situations I have previously sketched, the first area of conflict will be the changes involving worship.

On leaving theological college I served a curacy in a church where the incoming rector promised those who appointed him that he would never change anything during his incumbency. I did not realise this until I first led the 8.00 a.m. 1662 Communion Service. At this service between fifteen and twenty elderly worshippers sat in the four corners of a church which could seat five hundred.

I had been taking this service for a few weeks when I thought it might be helpful, in creating an atmosphere of fellowship, if I invited the congregation to take a more active part. In this service the minister usually started by praying the Lord's Prayer, followed by the prayer for purity of heart.

I invited the congregation to accompany me in these two prayers. Within a few days a small group visited the rector and requested that I be asked not to make such alterations in their service. I broke the rule once more when I asked if they would pray for one of their number who was ill in hospital. The majority had no idea who the sick person was, although she had attended the same service for probably twenty years.

Every church service, whether it be Catholic, Anglican or the most free house church, has some form of worship. One of our young people left the area to attend university. During his three years of academic study he joined a house church in the city where the worship and fellowship attracted many students. Each time the church assembled, the leadership sought to be free and open to the Holy Spirit's leading in the worship. Our friend noticed, however, during his three years with them, that the morning worship evolved into something remarkably similar to the Anglican Series III Communion Service. There was confession, the ministry of the word, intercessory prayer, worship culminating in a Eucharistic prayer of thanksgiving, etc.

If you can actually hear the words, you will find that the majority of popular songs today revolve around the 'love ballad'. It is popular because through words and music the artist or group are expressing the sentiments which many teenagers feel towards a particular boy or girl. By this first attraction to the opposite sex, the young people's emotions and desires are being stirred and they are wanting to express these feelings. When the Holy Spirit comes in power He has the same effect upon the followers of Jesus. They simply fall in love with Him in a new way, and want to express that love in words and music which are expressive of what they are feeling.

Such worship can involve the repetitive use of short songs. However, this is not new in inspired liturgical worship. When Solomon dedicated his newly built temple in Jerusalem and placed in it the Ark of the Lord, he organised a most impressive array of musicians and singers. It is written of the occasion that they sang the refrain: 'He is good; his love endures for ever' (2 Chronicles 5:13).

This song would hardly have been sung once, by such a large gathering of worship leaders. Voices and instruments would have combined enabling the worshippers to express their love for a God who they had discovered is both good and loving. The end of such worship is silence, as the presence of God filled the Temple. His glory, which means weight, was so present that nobody could move; they stood in awe and adoration.

If this was an integral part of worship under the old covenant, what should be our expectation under the new? Jesus taught the woman at the well in Samaria that there were three types of worship. She had pretended to be rather confused and asked Him where the right place to worship God was. Was it Mount Gerizim as the Samaritans maintained, or Jerusalem as advocated by the Jews? Jesus took the opportunity to tell her that she and her people worshipped in ignorance, implying that they did not know God, whereas the Jews did. They had the truth about God's nature revealed to them in the Scriptures. Jesus went on to say that His followers would worship God as Father 'in spirit and truth'. To worship in spirit means from a heart filled and motivated by the Holy Spirit. The Greek word most used for Christian worship means literally 'to come towards the kiss'. This is why so many of the new songs are love songs in which the worshipper expresses his love for Jesus.

Such innovation does not mean the abandonment of the hymns of the Christian tradition whose words at times go back to the earliest centuries and express the believers' love and devotion to Jesus. Rather, the Holy Spirit not only creates the new, but also illuminates and makes meaningful the old. However, when new styles of music are introduced, they cause as much consternation as the creative use of liturgy.

Choirs and organists are often a leader's greatest source of suffering and this can continue for many years and involve

him in local and national publicity. Of all the groups in a
church, the choir may have the most difficulty when the Holy
Spirit moves in power. Their musical tradition over many
decades has resisted any form of music considered to be
inferior. Choirs wield power within the established structures
and have often had little relationship with the congregation,
and none with the real spiritual ethos of the church. In one
church we visited, which is quite typical, the choir was almost
hidden from the congregation by a large, heavy, ornamental
rood screen installed in memory of some bygone dignitary.
The choir had a special door which led into the church and
also into their stalls, by which they arrived and left. This group
did not relate to or know the majority of the congregation
which they supposedly led in worship. Needless to say, they
opposed every new form of music which their vicar wanted
to introduce into the worship service.

We were once in a large parish church with a choir whose
pride was in its musical ability. Their music was broadcast.
When it was time to preach I climbed up into the pulpit and
was making some introductory remarks when I heard rustling
sounds behind me. Looking around I discovered the choir
members opening their Sunday newspapers. This took me so
much by surprise that it was a few moments before I could
get round to asking them if I was boring them! Needless to
say, the vicar had a difficult time as he started to introduce
more personal and intimate forms of worship.

As this style of worship is introduced it starts to open people
up to God. English people find it particularly difficult to
express any form of emotion. This is true in a service of
worship. Traditionally religion has been a private affair, and
in some quarters it is still thought to be rude to initiate a
conversation with someone you have not been introduced to.
Normally we keep feelings well and truly in check. The
barriers we create for our protection often hide deep areas
of hurt and fear. However, the true worship of God, expressed
in intimate love songs, is inclined to touch unresolved areas
and cause highly emotional and irrational responses. Again,

for the leader, this can be a harrowing experience to have to work through, as the person sees the cause of their reactions being the new songs rather than their emotional problems.

Besides people's opposition to this freedom in worship there is also a demonic reaction. The Devil has always sought to turn man away from God in acts of disobedience. This is what happened in the first encounter in the Garden of Eden (Genesis 3). The Devil will seek to hinder and oppose anything that will draw man into a closer, loving, committed relationship with Jesus. This is why the leaders of a church should always seek to protect their worship leaders as they, more than anyone else, receive the lashing from tongues inspired by the Devil.

Coupled with the changes in worship often goes the need to restructure the church to accommodate what is happening to the people. This can cause all manner of opposition which may border on the ridiculous.

I answered the telephone to hear a rather cultured voice, which I immediately identified as belonging to the vicar of a church we had visited six months previously. He came from a traditional background of public school and Oxbridge, and had attended an Anglo-Catholic theological college. For over twenty years he had gone through a religious routine and, in his own words, had never seen God do anything. He was now rector of a parish with an ancient church building incongruously set in the midst of a redeveloped area. God had moved in his life and the blessing had overflowed into a number of his church members. He usually celebrated Holy Communion with his back to the congregation, the nearest of whom was about twenty yards away. He could hardly see half of them as they were spread out to the right and left of the main body of the church. With this new-found vision he wanted 'the body' of church members to become more of a fellowship and experience the new life together. To facilitate this he put a wooden, movable altar at the top of the chancel steps. This meant that he could see and be seen by the whole congregation. Within days it was as if all hell had been let loose.

John started to outline the problems he was having with a number of powerful individuals who were aggressively opposing what he was doing. This situation caused him to have a number of sleepless nights. The reasons given by the opposition were varied. Some maintained that because people had worshipped at the altar since the eleventh century the vicar had no right to change the tradition. Others thought that to bring the altar down brought God too close. However, one of the most amazing reasons might have come from the world of Roald Dahl. A number of ladies had sat together in the same pew for over three decades and had always counted thirty-nine paces to reach the altar rails. Any diminution of paces was too traumatic for them to contemplate. They said that they would be extremely uncomfortable if God were any closer.

If I had recorded all such experiences related to me by clergy, then a larger book than this would be required. However, the case of a Hampshire vicar is a classic. Under his long ministry many young couples and community leaders had been converted to Christ, including the headmaster of the local school. The vicar, aged sixty-nine, was a real Caleb. He had been incumbent of the church for twenty-six years and was well respected, both in the community he served and the diocese. He found the interior structure of the church inadequate to express the new spiritual life. He wanted to create more space, to bring the 'altar' down into the congregation and replace the pews with movable chairs. The opposition (many were not regular churchgoers at all) was led by a man elected as a churchwarden who eventually took the vicar to the Consistory Court. Reporters assembled in the parish hall as the Chancellor and lawyers considered the situation. After all sides had submitted their case, the Chancellor ruled in favour of maintaining the historic structures. Embracing the cross, the vicar called the church to pursue a way of peace. He told reporters that he had no intention of doing anything but forgiving and loving the opposition.

Another need for change within the worshipping congregation is to accommodate those whom the Holy Spirit is drawing to Jesus from a wide variety of backgrounds and situations. Many of these people are 'unchurched'. They have a powerful and life-changing experience of the Holy Spirit, and need to belong to a congregation where this can be understood and expressed.

Jonathan came from a middle-class family and was educated in the public school system. He left school to pursue an art course. After two-and-a-half years he dropped out and went to live in a squat in Brixton. Here he smoked pot and was soon main-lining heroin. Being musical he formed a punk band and, when sober enough, played in various clubs and pubs. Some four years later he developed severe hepatitis and his doctors gave him three months to live unless he radically altered his lifestyle. Whilst recovering from this illness, he went to a number of clinics to 'dry out' but always returned to the needle. In desperation his parents arranged a series of consultations for him with an eminent psychiatrist who specialised in drug-related problems. All this was to no avail. His distraught parents took him home to live with them. They had arranged to go on holiday, but felt unable to go until Jonathan had found a safe place to stay. As a result he arranged to visit Steve, an old school and family friend who lived in Devon. A few years previously Steve had become a Christian.

Jonathan had only been staying a short time when Steve started to tell him about Jesus and His power to free. Jonathan was going through withdrawal symptoms at the time and was not at all impressed. However, Steve's love and sharing were a persistent, challenging message which Jonathan was unable to ignore; it started to penetrate.

One evening, in desperation, Jonathan called to Jesus for help. He subsequently said that he was unable to put into words what actually happened. Suffice it to say, incredible power flowed through his mind and body, charging him with an electricity-type energy. From that moment his heroin dependence stopped and an inner healing process started. Three years later Jonathan is still free from drug addiction. His experience of freedom and joy could not be expressed in traditional terms of worship. He had a joy unspeakable which came from a heart full of thanksgiving and praise.

My friend the late Bishop Timoteus of the Marthoma Church had a diocese in Kerala, a state in South West India. He came to stay with us during a conference hosted by St Andrew's. He spent long nights on the floor of his bedroom, cross-legged in prayer. Having asked for prayer on the final night he awoke at 2 a.m. to pray again and during this time became filled with the Holy Spirit. He greeted me in the morning with, 'Barry, what am I going to do with all this power?' His concern was how he could express this new-found joy in the structure of the Marthoma Church.

Chapter 10

THE POWER FACTOR

On one occasion I was visiting a city in North America. Whilst there I heard of a church which had a large, eclectic congregation and in which it was rumoured that the Holy Spirit was ministering in great power. Being free on the Sunday evening, I made my way there. On the train I sat next to a young man who was crippled and walked with difficulty. As we chatted I discovered that he was going to the same meeting, so I asked whether I could accompany him.

We arrived to find the large auditorium buzzing with excitement. A choir accompanied by an orchestra were singing Gospel songs. Eventually we came to the sermon, which was biblical and long. As it finished the preacher ministered in what has come to be termed 'the power of the Holy Spirit'. He started by calling out to the front all those who were poor. My friend struggled to his feet and joined the other sixty or more people. The preacher told them it was not God's intention for anyone who believed in Jesus to be poor, so he broke the power of their poverty, and called upon the Lord to make them all very rich. After this, those concerned returned to their seats and the sick were invited to receive their healing. My friend had hardly returned to his seat when he was on his way to the front once again. We were told that Jesus was present to heal everyone, and if it was not happening for you, it was either because of your sin or lack of faith. My friend did not go forward when the Lord was healing the demonised, as he had run out of energy.

To my mind what happened that evening was a gross distortion of the Gospel. It was triumphalism at its worst. There seemed to be no cross or place for suffering. The impression was given that the preacher had God's words on the situation and if it did not happen for you, then the fault was yours not God's. This is an extreme illustration. However, one of the main dangers of the renewed emphasis on ministering in the power of the Holy Spirit is to overlook or by-pass the message of the cross. Without this message we are left with a 'candy coated Gospel', sweet tasting but devoid of reality.

It would seem that swirling around the cross are many powerful currents which intermingle such as victory over sin, forgiveness, deliverance from evil, reconciliation and healing. Yet at the same time there are currents of suffering which are not alleviated and, ultimately, death which at the time is without meaning to those most closely involved. Only in the light of the resurrection do we glimpse a perspective which gives us hope in every eventuality of life.

The message of the cross can only be understood by those who have a child-like perception of spiritual truth. Its inherent power cannot be comprehended through intellectual wisdom or knowledge. To such people the message of the cross is foolishness. The word that Paul uses here is particularly descriptive. In Greek it is μωρια ('moria') which we translate as moronic. Paul is saying that the message of the cross is something that an adult with a mental age of a child could have thought up. However, to those who receive its message, the cross is the power of God to bring wholeness (1 Corinthians 1:17–18).

It was Paul's experience that, when he preached the message of the cross, it was accompanied by a powerful ministry by the Holy Spirit. He made real in the hearers' lives all that the cross symbolised in order that their faith might be in God's power alone. He writes:

When I came to you, brothers, I did not come with

eloquence or superior wisdom as I proclaimed to you the testimony about God. For I resolved to know nothing while I was with you except Jesus Christ and him crucified. I came to you in weakness and fear, and with much trembling. My message and my preaching were not with wise and persuasive words but with demonstration of the Spirit's power, so that your faith might not rest on men's wisdom, but on God's power (1 Corinthians 2:1–5).

Basic to this ministry is the realisation that those who proclaim the message of the cross have nothing within themselves that can elicit wholeness and new life in others. No amount of intellectual reasoning will do it, nor will natural eloquence. Such power can only rest upon human weakness and vulnerability. However, where such conditions prevail it is essential that we are able to hear God telling us what He is doing in a situation or a person's life. The problem of application revolves around the promises of Jesus on the one hand and our understanding of His will on the other.

In John 10 Jesus takes the well-known sight of a shepherd with his flock to illustrate His relationship with His disciples. He, Jesus, is the Good Shepherd, and He says that 'the sheep listen to his voice' (v.3) again 'they know his voice' (v.4). This implies that in the area of guidance the believer will be able to hear the Lord. He makes a similar statement in John 14 when He speaks of the Holy Spirit who is to come. He will 'teach you all things' (John 14:26), 'guide you into all truth' (John 16:13). This was certainly true of the Christians after the coming of the Holy Spirit at Pentecost.

Although what Jesus has said is true, the problem we have is really hearing God. Unfortunately, there is no hot line to the Almighty. In the situations in which I have been totally wrong it is either the result of my insensitivity or accepting as coming from God what my own thoughts, feelings and emotions were telling me. However, the bottom line is that God does speak, and it is part of the cost to be prepared to be wrong in order that God may help people through you.

Such occasions can be painful.

We were invited by the churches of Aylesbury to lead a mission to the town. Don Brewin, vicar of Holy Trinity, had initially approached us. My colleague, Iain Roberts, and I had subsequently met the fourteen church leaders to pray and prepare for the outreach to the town. Together, we decided to hold a week of meetings in people's homes, to be followed by three nights in the Town Hall with a final Celebration in the indoor stadium at Stoke Mandeville. Two months prior to the outreach, one of our team leaders met with those who planned to open their homes for the hundred meetings which were planned. It was envisaged that one of our team would join one of theirs to lead these meetings. At the end of a study course I was to speak to a gathering of all the churches in a large, central venue. This was to prove a very difficult evening for me as I made a great error of judgment.

The day before the central meeting I had been for two weeks with a team at Holy Trinity, Parr Mount, which is a parish on the edge of St Helens in Merseyside. It is a working class parish with a large percentage of people unemployed. In a recent survey it was designated a 'high priority' area by the government. Chris Wood, a fellow New Zealander, and his wife, Cathy, had, through many traumas, been instrumental in introducing renewal to the church. Our two weeks with them saw a culmination of their three years of prayer and hard work. The first week was based on homes where neighbours and friends were invited to talk about Jesus. During the second week we had larger gatherings centred on the church. These meetings were entitled 'God in Action', which aptly described what actually happened. Each evening, after worship, testimony and preaching, we invited the Holy Spirit to minister to those present. On some occasions His coming had been extremely gentle, whilst at others He had come in great power. By the end of the two weeks many testified to finding a faith in Jesus Christ, whilst others experienced a variety of healings in their lives. It was from this situation that I had come straight to Aylesbury.

The beautiful old parish church was packed to capacity; the music team led us in an inspiring act of worship, after which I spoke. In my closing remarks I asked all those gathered to stand and welcome the Holy Spirit to minister. Evidently many people were acutely embarrassed by this. A number of leaders suggested that someone else be asked to preach at the public meetings that were to follow. It was Don Brewin, as chairman, who eventually made peace with those opposed to my continuing.

I had been hurt by people's negative reactions to me, but it was a hurt I had brought upon myself through insensitivity. I was on a 'high' and ministered in Aylesbury as if it was the final evening of a series of meetings at Holy Trinity, Parr Mount. I had not, through teaching and testimony, prepared the people for any new things the Holy Spirit might be wanting to do. In this instance I needed to repent, not only of insensitivity but also of self-pity, which was the actual basis of my hurt.

I have found as an evangelist that the more I allow the Holy Spirit the opportunity to minister, the greater is the negative come-back. Whilst a final year student at theological college, I preached three sermons. The last one was in a rather traditional church. I preached on the message of the cross under the title of 'New Life in Jesus'. I concluded by inviting anyone who was not experiencing the new life of which I spoke to talk with me at the end of the service. To my surprise a teenager from the choir sought me out. I prayed with him and gave him a Gospel of Mark and a booklet on Christian beginnings. The general comment from the church leader was that such an ending to a sermon was quite unnecessary, as everyone in the church was a Christian.

This was the first of many criticisms I received over the years regarding the preaching of the message of the cross and the inviting of a response. Although I was never taught it at theological college, I have come to realise that such suffering is to be expected by a minister of the Gospel.

However, it was not until I started invoking the Holy Spirit

that I experienced the hurt of being misunderstood. After
preaching on the cross I would ask the Holy Spirit to come
and confirm the message. The main difficulty in such a
ministry is that, whenever the Holy Spirit is invoked, there
is no way one can guarantee what happens. It is a shock to
discover that His ways are not our ways, nor His thoughts
our thoughts. As Christians we have sought to control God;
we have done this by adhering to a rigid form of liturgical
worship which regulates what happens in the tradition of our
church. This is not just a problem in western Europe.

One morning before a conference in Africa I rose early to
pray. Sitting outside I watched as the sun rose over the hills,
casting its lengthening rays on the fields and spotlighting the
houses which nestled on the slopes. It was a glorious morning;
praise and thanksgiving to God flowed from my lips as I
responded to His creation. When I came to read the Psalms
they too were alive with the presence and goodness of God.
It was one of those mornings when I wished that I had risen
earlier. As I had not, I longed for time to stand still, so that
I could spend my day locked in that moment.

The stillness was broken as, from the verandah, I was called
to join the team for breakfast. After eating I went to my room
to collect some notes before going to the conference. Suddenly
I was overwhelmed by a feeling of great sadness. It felt like
the kind of sorrow a lover would feel if rejected by the one
he loved. I tried to analyse my feelings. Although Mary was
not with me on the trip I knew that it did not apply to our
relationship. It seemed to me as if I was somehow experiencing
the sorrow of the Holy Spirit.

The pastor who was organising the meeting wanted me to
outline in detail exactly how I would conduct it. As far as I
was able, I did. He put a constriction on the ministry by
requesting that, if the sick were prayed for, then I alone would
do it, and not the team. I consented to this and we prayed
together.

As a theme I had taken John the Baptist's description of
the ministry of Jesus, showing that He was both the Lamb

of God who took away the sin of the world, and also the one who baptised with the Holy Spirit. I developed both these strands and ended up with Jesus' invitation to receive the Holy Spirit when He said, 'If anyone is thirsty, let him come to me and drink. Whoever believes in me, as the Scripture has said, streams of living water will flow from within him' (John 7:37-38).

To prepare the people for His coming I reminded them that the Father delighted to give the Holy Spirit to those who asked Him. All we needed to do was receive. As people began to ask, the Holy Spirit started to fall upon individuals. Many words of knowledge were given and people responded by walking to the front. I started to pray when suddenly the minister stood up and requested everybody to return to their seats. As he did this the sorrow I had felt earlier in the morning returned. He then proceeded to tell the congregation that I was an instrument of the Devil, and what I was teaching and doing was his work. His harangue lasted for ten minutes or more. An awful gloom descended on the congregation. After he had finished he asked me if I would like to say anything. I realised that this was no place for self-justification, but rather to accept the way of the cross, so I declined.

I have often been criticised by those who consider what happens at their church during visits as being too emotional. This is because on occasions people will express emotions when the Holy Spirit comes upon them. I sometimes find this type of manifestation embarrassing and wish I could be somewhere else when it happens. But I know from experience what a transforming experience it can be for those involved. The following is a typical example of what I mean. During the ministering time the Holy Spirit fell upon a woman. She was in her early forties, and adopted. However, this had not been communicated to her until she was ten and then in adverse circumstances. She had had an argument with her father and in a fit of temper he told her that he would send her back where she belonged if she did not behave herself. It was then she learnt she was adopted. She had immediately

Another Way

suppressed this truth and had never allowed herself to think about it for over thirty years. When the Holy Spirit touched her this deep shock was released through piercing screams. I tried to encourage her to reduce the decibels, as I could see the effect it was having on a number of regular worshippers. However, my overtures were in vain, and she became louder before collapsing across the pew. Many people find such behaviour offensive in a church setting. People often say that it is not respectable. It may be that we mistakenly equate 'respectability' with 'goodness'.

One of the main difficulties is that the Church in western Europe has absorbed the secular materialistic values of the society in which it is situated. This society sees man as the centre of the universe with the intellectual resources to overcome all problems. Modern man judges all things from the confines of his mind. A thing is true if it can be proved by scientific experimentation. The infiltration of this philosophy has had the result of making the Church anti-supernatural. Spiritual phenomena are judged according to the understandings of the rational mind and, as a result, are dismissed. This is why the divinity of Christ, His miracles, His bodily resurrection and ascension are reinterpreted to fit into what the mind can accept as being possible. It is almost as if this liberal position has been proved to be right as, until recently, we have seen little of the miraculous working of the Holy Spirit in power. On the other hand, most of our conservative theologians, when treating the subject of the Holy Spirit, give more attention to His person than to His power, who He is rather than what He does. But the Holy Spirit does not want to be known as a person; rather, His main concern is that through His works Jesus will be made known.

Because of the lack of spiritual power in the churches, we have a restricted view of the Holy Spirit as being a gentleman. We give the impression that He is always the gentle, gracious dove who would never cause embarrassment, and always act in secret. If only that were so!

On one occasion we were waiting for the Lord before a

meeting when one of our team shared a most extraordinary
revelation. She said that she had seen a picture of a fist
knocking people out. From this she concluded that the Holy
Spirit was going to knock many people out that evening. I
did not comment as I thought it was a little far fetched to have
any significance. At the end of the meeting, whilst waiting
for the Holy Spirit to minister, I perceived that He was
anointing many people for ministry. I invited those who
recognised the presence of the Holy Spirit upon them to come
to the front of the hall, explaining that our team would pray
with them. About thirty responded, and as they came to
within about twenty feet of the stage, they fell to the ground.
Nobody had touched them and I had not suggested that this
would happen. As they lay on the ground the anointing Spirit
came powerfully upon them. I wondered whether Paul had
a similar experience when knocked to the ground.

Whilst ministering in Palmerston North, during a tour of
New Zealand, I saw the Holy Spirit work in a surprising way.
Debbie, a young member of our team, told me that she
discerned that the Lord wanted to minister to people with back
problems. Consequently I suggested that those with back
conditions, who would like prayer for healing, should assemble
at the front of the church. I thought that there would probably
be half a dozen at the most, and was surprised when nearly
thirty came forward. Debbie invited the Holy Spirit to
minister to this group and as she did so I noticed Him come
powerfully on a man who was standing with his back to me.
Initially he had difficulty standing upright; he was a large
man, dressed in summer shorts and sweatshirt. As I watched
he was visibly stretched – it was as if he was being held under
his arms and periodically being lifted a few inches above the
ground. Some people find it difficult when the Holy Spirit
moves in such overt ways, but I find it equally difficult when
there is no visible manifestation of His presence.

We were invited by a committee representing many
missionary societies working in East Africa to lead their annual
conference at Kumbaya. Prior to this we had a week in

Gahini, a hilltop mission station in Rwanda. During this visit we led a day's conference on a nearby hill. When we arrived we found chairs and forms put out on the edge of a banana plantation.

As the drums sounded people gathered from all over the hillside. By the time we started about two hundred men, women and children made up an ever-increasing circle. They led off with songs of worship and our team followed. I then spoke on the signs of the Kingdom. I taught that the Kingdom of God was a Kingdom of spiritual power, and that its coming could be observed. We could see its presence following the preaching of the cross through conversion to Jesus, healing, exorcism, the raising of the dead, the gifts of the Holy Spirit, celebration and, finally, suffering. I ended by saying that the power of this Kingdom was the Holy Spirit.

It took a while to communicate this message, as often my interpreter would stop and have a little discussion as to what I was actually trying to say. But these were not the only interruptions. Every so often the crowd would break into song, praising the name of Jesus for what I had mentioned He did. Then came the time of ministry.

I invited them to stand and explained how we would invite the Holy Spirit to minister to us. As I watched it did not seem as if anything was happening. They stood quietly, looking straight ahead. I started to feel selfconscious and embarrassed. We had two words of knowledge: the first to the effect that there were people who were terrified to walk along certain paths by the forest; the second was to the effect that a number suffered from leg conditions. I invited those concerned to come forward. Our team prayed and nothing, absolutely nothing observable, happened. Those being prayed with just stood and stared. Finally the meeting closed.

We had lunch (a piece of bread and a drink) in a little mud hut which doubled as a chapel. Afterwards another team member taught on the gifts of the Holy Spirit. At the end of a long, hot afternoon the local pastor invited those who had been helped to stand and share their testimony.

I was truly amazed as we heard of the powerful things the Holy Spirit had done. Many testified to feeling the presence of fear leave them. The joy of this was such that they started to dance and sing. A number of men testified to receiving the healing of their legs. One in particular said that he had had very limited use of his right leg and, as the power came upon him, he was freed. Yet there had been no obvious sign of His presence.

However, some manifestations of His power can be disturbing, and there is one gift in particular which causes all sorts of controversy. An old friend of mine, who holds the gifts of the Holy Spirit at arm's length, once remarked that if you say there is someone in any given meeting with a problem with head, stomach or back, then you can guarantee a response. He is right; that is why I have always found ministering the word of knowledge in a church situation, or to individuals, difficult.

Cynics will suggest that God could not possibly be interested in the throbbing toe of a middle-class stockbroker, whilst millions are dying of starvation in Africa. Some observe that, as we grow older, we have to live with our degenerative aches and pains. Others remark that words of knowledge are embarrassing and make the church introverted. Besides all that, I have been accused of having occult powers such as would be exercised by mediums.

On one occasion I was invited to give the Bible Study at a British Youth for Christ staff retreat. This was to be held at the London Bible College. During prayers that morning a man, whom I had only seen once, and never spoken to, came into my mind. As I was thinking about him my thoughts were drawn back to Habakkuk, chapter 2, a Scripture which I had memorised. 'The Lord gave me this answer: "Write down clearly on clay tablets what I reveal to you, so that it can be read at a glance. Put it in writing, because it is not yet time for it to come true. But the time is coming quickly, and what I show you will come true. It may seem slow in coming, but wait for it; it will certainly take place, and it will not be delayed.'' ' (Good News Bible).

I felt that the Lord was telling me to write to this man and enclose the Scripture. Before I went to the London Bible College I discovered his name and address, so on the way I posted the letter. I was rather embarrassed doing this as I had received such letters myself from well-meaning people who thought that they were conveying a special message to me from God. These messages often seemed to have no relevance at all to my situation especially when they contained rather strange pictures from the book of Revelation. As I drove in to the college car park I was thinking how fortunate it was that I did not have to meet him and deliver the message personally.

After the Bible study we broke for coffee and, as I went into the corridor outside the lecture room, whom should I see but the man for whom I had the message, Clifford Hill. Unbeknown to me, he was to lead the remainder of the day. My heart started to pound and I felt extremely selfconscious. Initially I did not think I would mention the word of knowledge, or the letter which was probably already on the way to his home. We smiled and he made his way ahead of me to the coffee area. I was not staying for the day and was just about to leave when the Scripture again flashed into my mind. Taking courage in both hands, I stopped him and told him I had a message from God for him. Shortly after this I left and never saw him again.

A number of years later I was in W. H. Smith, the booksellers, browsing through their recent publications. My eye was caught by a book whose title, *Towards the Dawn*, intrigued me. I noticed that Clifford Hill was its author. Out of curiosity I turned to the author's preface. To my absolute amazement, I began to read about the meeting we had together at the London Bible College. That 'word', passed to him outside the coffee room, was the sign which led him to write the book.

On other occasions it has been even harder to give such words. One morning whilst waiting upon the Lord, a woman whose name I did not know came to mind. All I knew about her was that she was a critic of St Andrew's, although she had never been there. As I started to pray for her I was given an insight into her life and situation. It seemed to me as if the Lord wanted me to visit her with a message. I was simply to tell her that Jesus knew her situation and loved her. For a number of days I put off the inevitable but eventually I made my way with trepidation to her front door and knocked. My initial reception was frosty. I mumbled away on the doorstep for what seemed ages before she reluctantly invited me in.

For ten minutes we talked about generalities; I had taken a church magazine with me and was just about to offer it and take my leave when I was reminded of the purpose for my visit. Again, with hesitancy and apprehension, I told her that God knew her situation and that Jesus loved her. To my surprise she received this and we were able to talk about her situation.

It is encouraging to remember situations which have positive conclusions. However, there are many that apparently do not. These are even more embarrassing. Even as I write, I remember with anguish the times I have spoken words I supposed were from the Lord to people who have just stared back at me, engulfing us both in an awkward silence!

Ministering the word of knowledge outside a church situation is difficult, but within weekly Sunday services it is even more fraught with misunderstandings and negative responses. At St Andrew's we started by being open to receive words of knowledge at the prayer meetings prior to the services. Here David would ask those present to share anything that they sensed God might want to do in the lives of people attending the services. A list was made and then read out prior to the blessing. For those who led the service, this was the most embarrassing moment in the worship.

After a year we decided that, instead of seeking these words prior to the service, we would integrate this time of waiting upon God into the service, and receive the revelations directly from the congregation. We first introduced this in the evening service, and eventually into the morning.

We, as leaders, found this ministry difficult in two main areas. It is our custom to invite the Holy Spirit to show us, through the words of knowledge, any condition that He wants to minister to. We wait upon the Lord for some moments, then encourage people to speak out what they are receiving. The leader then relays their revelations to the congregation through the microphone. It is at this moment one feels stupid and embarrassed; one wonders what normal, rational people are thinking as one relays back to the congregation some apparently insignificant condition.

Harder still to deal with are the criticisms from people one respects. Some suggest that we limit this gift to Home Groups so that it will only involve people of a like mind. Our problem is that we believe that God wants us to minister in this way, as it is one of the ways, we believe, by which Jesus knew what the Father wanted Him to do. On occasions we would have been happy to abolish this ministry, but we knew we could not. This means we need to know the power of the cross and the dying to self each time before we minister.

The same applies to the gift of prophecy. I have exercised the gift of tongues in private prayer for nearly twenty-five years. However, to speak publicly in tongues always means reflecting on the cross before speaking. Running through my mind will be many questions: what will people think when they hear a language spoken which they do not know? How do those who do not believe in such manifestations respond when they hear? What if there is no one in the meeting with the gift of interpretation? What if the word I sense I am being given is just from my own imagination?

Once I have spoken out, there is the waiting for an interpretation. For those who have spoken in tongues, this can seem an eternity as they wait to be justified in the utterance they have made. I have also had the same experience when prophesying in English. However, I am encouraged by the word of the Scripture which says that we are to 'eagerly desire' this particular gift (1 Corinthians 14:1).

On occasions people will tell me that they found a particular prophecy 'trite' or 'simplistic'. It was saying something that is basic to scriptural revelation. On the one hand I would agree, but on the other Scripture tells us 'not to treat prophecy with contempt'. In fact, one of the most profound prophecies given to the people of Israel returning from Babylonian exile was from Haggai when the Lord simply said, 'I am with you'.

A lady once stopped me in the street to tell me that my ministry was divisive. She said that her church had been perfectly all right until we visited. Since that time there had been divisions in the choir and groupings within the church. She was echoing what I find the most difficult part of ministering in the power of the Holy Spirit. Inevitably there will be divisions because the ministry of Jesus is divisive. He said that He had not come to bring peace, but a sword. He would even divide families.

On one occasion Jesus was teaching about His uniqueness. He claimed that, unless people fed upon Him as the bread of life, they would not experience eternal life. Many found such teaching offensive and ceased to follow Him. Often His powerful acts of exorcism were attributed to the Devil, whereas His healings caused all sorts of problems for the religious people of His day. In this context I note how contemporary are people's reactions to His healing of the man born blind. John writes that Jesus took the initiative with the young man concerned and, having put a saliva-based mud on his eyelids, told him to wash in the nearby pool. Instantly sight was restored. The Pharisees said that the miracle could not possibly be of God because it happened on the Sabbath. The Jews thought it was a hoax as they did not believe that the man was born blind; they disregarded any possibility of Jesus having healed him because, in their opinion, Jesus was a sinner. The healing has a sad ending as the leaders expelled the young man from their synagogue (John 9).

We are bidden in the Scriptures not to quench the Holy Spirit. Those of us in a position of leadership do this when, through fear or unbelief, we will not make a way for the Holy

Spirit to minister. This attitude reflects our unpreparedness
to accept the suffering which allowing the Holy Spirit space
would involve. Many instances come to mind, but one which
is fresh happened recently in East Africa.

At a Sunday morning worship service our team shared and
I spoke on the cross as being the power of God. I majored
on the themes of reconciliation, deliverance from evil, and
healing. When the meeting officially ended, everyone
remained seated. Initially a number testified to the power of
the cross. This was followed by spontaneous praising and
dancing. Eventually everyone sat and a stillness came upon
the meeting.

A man stood up and said he would like to ask a question.
It was rhetorical. Why was it that nobody wanted to leave
the meeting? He waited for a few minutes and then said that
it was because the Holy Spirit was present in power. I felt
that this power of the Lord was present for healing the sick.
I asked my interpreter if he would relay this to the pastor,
with a request that we be allowed to minister healing in the
name of Jesus. The answer came back in the negative. He
was too fearful to allow God to work in this way. His
reluctance to risk his reputation as a senior churchman
overrode his obedience to the Holy Spirit who, on this
occasion, was quenched. The people in Jesus' home town also
quenched Him through their unbelief.

The Holy Spirit has been given to the Church, but we must
allow space for Him to minister and this is when we must
be prepared to be a fool for Christ. The prophet Joel writes
of the Holy Spirit being 'poured out' upon God's people (Joel
2:28). It is a metaphor which is descriptive of water. When
water is poured it usually falls in an indiscriminate way. It
is the leader's function, through the guidance of the Holy
Spirit, to open all the channels so the 'water' may pour
through.

If the African pastor had given his permission, we would
have ministered through words of knowledge, and then invited
all who would like healing prayer to come to a place where

our team could minister to them

On one occasion I was thinking about people's reactions to the power of God when my thoughts drifted to a period of my life when I was living in Jordan. Sometimes for a break we would journey from Damascus over the Lebanese mountains to Beirut. The journey was always awe-inspiring; often there would be snow on the mountains. As the narrow road wound down through the villages towards the coast, the famous cedars gave way to the vineyards whose vines were cultivated to grow close to the ground, so their leaves would hide the dew from the burning sun.

Halfway down the scent of oranges heralded the beginning of the citrus fruits. Between the orchards and the city itself were the numerous market gardens. Beirut was cosmopolitan, with its fine French architecture and bustling Arab bazaars. The business area and smart hotels radiated wealth and success.

Recently I saw television pictures from Beirut; they were of Palestinian children who had been born within the confines of the refugee camps. These camps had often been under siege and all that was left in many instances were ruined homes and surroundings. If I had met these children and described the Beirut I knew, they would have looked at me with disbelief. They had all been born amongst the ruins, and knew nothing of the wonder and beauty that had once been Lebanon.

The majority of us have lived our lives in the ruins of the Church. We have accepted as normal the musty traditions, the dwindling elderly female congregations, and the lack of power or relevance. We have appointed ecclesiastical committees for closing down churches and disposing of property. We have created nothing that will help us deal with growth and expansion. It is no wonder that when God moves in supernatural power there is division, for what was normal at the beginning of the Church's life has, in our time, become the abnormal.

However, there is a way for a church leader who, under

God, wants to bring his congregation into an experience of freedom and spiritual normality. But it is the way of the cross. James and his brother, John, asked Jesus whether they could be at His right hand in the Kingdom. Jesus replied that their request was not in His jurisdiction to grant. However, they could be baptised with the baptism that He was baptised with (Mark 10:38). This was a twofold baptism; it was a baptism of power, but also of suffering. Those who follow the cross will experience both.

Chapter 11

SHARING JESUS

The face of Britain has changed beyond recognition since I arrived here from New Zealand nearly thirty years ago. During these years immigrants like myself have arrived, many from India, Pakistan, Africa and the Caribbean. Each group has brought not only its unique culture, but also its religion. These range from belief in one god to many. Large areas of our cities, which once had a nominal Christian presence, now have churches struggling to survive whilst nearby mosques and Hindu temples are often full to overflowing.

The Church has found it difficult to understand or meet this challenge. One of the effects of this has been to view all religions as being equally valid and as different ways in which man approaches the one God. Canterbury Cathedral, home of the English Church, recently hosted the 'Canterbury Festival of Faith and the Environment'. An information sheet outlined the purpose of the gathering:

On the Saturday night, in the darkened interior of the great Cathedral, a new celebration in music, dance, sound and symbol will be performed. Drawing upon the architecture of the Cathedral itself, and upon the teachings and beliefs of many faiths, you are invited to celebrate the Forest as one of the most vital and most threatened of the aspects of nature. Throughout the Festival, Buddhists, Muslims, Christians, Baha'is, Jews, Sikhs and Hindus will celebrate, each in their own way, their care for nature through special acts of worship and prayer which will take place at various sites around the city. On Sunday morning an ecumenical liturgy will be celebrated at the Cathedral by the Archbishop of Canterbury.

The holding of multi-faith celebrations is not uncommon in our major cathedrals. Winchester hosted such a gathering prior to Canterbury, where all faiths made a covenant with God, with one another, and with nature, called the Rainbow Covenant.

In 1982 the Church of England invited nine Anglican leaders from nine countries to join with other Church representatives from home and abroad to take an in-depth look at the Church. Their prophetic report, *To a Rebellious House*, makes depressing reading, but the saddest aspect was the visitors' inability to discover a Gospel within the Church. They wrote that 'The difficulty experienced in reaching mutual understanding and agreement about evangelism is one of the most serious questions facing the Church of England.' We need once again to recapture a confidence in the Good News about Jesus.

It is important to realise that the early church congregations were founded in cultures which, like ours, paid homage to many gods and goddesses. Religions abounded. To such a church, situated in Rome, Paul wrote, 'I am not ashamed of the gospel, because it is the power of God for the salvation of everyone who believes: first for the Jew, then for the Gentile. For in the gospel a righteousness from God is revealed, a righteousness that is by faith from first to last, just as it is written, ''The righteous will live by faith'' ' (Romans 1:16–17).

We need to grasp the fact that the God who created all men became the man Jesus Christ. He is the one who sacrificed His life to pay the penalty for the sins of all mankind. He rose again and is coming a second time to be the judge of all men, whether they are religious, atheist or agnostic. It was this conviction which sent men and women from this country

to plant the Church in practically every country in the world.
To a New Zealander, Christmas Day 1814 is particularly
significant. It was on that day that Samuel Marsden, a
Yorkshire clergyman, sailed into the Bay of Islands where his
ship *Active* anchored in the beautiful Whangaroa Harbour.
Going ashore, Marsden preached the Gospel of Christ for the
first time. Ruatara, a Maori Christian whom he befriended
in Australia, translated. The results were powerful and far-
reaching. A. H. Reed, the New Zealand historian, wrote that
twenty years after Marsden's first visit, 'The killing of babies,
the murder of slaves at the passing of a chief, and even
cannibal feasts, were becoming less frequent' and that 'Chiefs,
who waged a victorious war, had killed and eaten many of
their enemies and enslaved others, changed the habits of a
lifetime, liberated their slaves and sent them back free men
to take the Gospel of Peace to their own people.'

It is in this powerful Good News – that Jesus Christ can
radically change lives – that we need to regain our
confidence. In the ancient world, Corinth was known as one
of the most notorious cities. A 'Corinthian girl' was the name
by which prostitutes were known. The city had a variety of
temples where contact with the gods was made through a
secular relationship: temple prostitutes included both men and
women. It was into this city that Paul took the message of
the crucified Jesus. He expressed his own conviction about
the power of the cross in these terms: 'For the message of the
cross is foolishness to those who are perishing, but to us who
are being saved it is the power of God' (1 Corinthians 1:18).

In this city of blatant sin and evil, many people turned to
Christ and experienced His power to change their lives.
Wanting his new converts to reflect on what they had been
changed from, Paul wrote a letter to them in which he asked
the question:

> Do you not know that the wicked will not inherit the
> kingdom of God? Do not be deceived: neither the sexually
> immoral nor idolaters nor adulterers nor male prostitutes

nor homosexual offenders nor thieves nor the greedy nor
drunkards nor slanderers nor swindlers will inherit the
kingdom of God. And that is what some of you were. But
you were washed, you were sanctified, you were justified
in the name of the Lord Jesus Christ and by the Spirit of
our God. (1 Corinthians 6:9–11)

In preparing a local church to evangelise, the first mistake
that is often made is to talk about it! There is nothing more
frightening or threatening than to expect people to share what
is thought to be private and, often, unformulated. Evangelism
is a believer's spontaneous response to his experience of Jesus
Christ.

Recently I was talking to a nurse who had, three months
previously, become a Christian. In the course of our
conversation I asked her how this had happened. She told me
that it was through the witness of her brother. This helps to
illustrate my point.

Paul was in his late twenties, and all his life had been a
drifter. He ended up driving a taxi in a market town. One
of his fares was an elderly lady. Paul was a chain-smoker and
asked her if she minded if he smoked. She replied that she
most certainly did mind, then proceeded to tell him how she
too had been a chain-smoker. He asked her how she had been
able to stop, to which she replied: 'By the power of the Lord
Jesus.' This encounter was eventually to lead him to faith in
Christ.

The spiritual life in the congregation from which the elderly
lady came had been revitalised by the Holy Spirit: this is a
prerequisite to evangelism. Such a fresh work by the Spirit
is usually the result of a congregation making prayer and
worship its first priority.

Regular meetings for prayer will affect the congregation
in a number of ways. Its immediate result will be to raise
people's level of faith and create an atmosphere of expectancy.
It will also make individuals aware of their own spiritual
needs. This in turn can lead to a seeking after the 'living

water' of the Spirit, of which Jesus spoke.

Paul's new-found relationship with Christ had two phases.
It started when he was witnessed to from the back of his taxi.
The second was when the elderly lady invited him to
accompany her to church. He said that it was among her
congregation that he had seen and experienced the life-
changing power of Christ.

I have a friend who is a successful car salesman. He takes
every opportunity to commend his product to any sympathetic
listener. If in the course of discussion the listener's interest
grows, he suggests that they visit his showroom and see for
themselves the car which he has eulogised.

As Christians we ought to be able to take people with whom
we have shared our faith to our services. Here they can expect
to see and experience the new life in Christ which we have
described. This would include relevant worship, teaching,
prayer, fellowship, and an opportunity to be prayed with for
whatever their particular need might be.

From a church which is being spiritually awakened comes
a confidence in the Gospel of Christ. As worshippers
encounter Him and experience His healing and freeing power,
they realise that the same Jesus can meet the needs of their
friends and colleagues. Evangelism ceases to be an 'ought'
and becomes a pleasure and a joy.

As the Holy Spirit awakens the church there is much more
for the regular worshippers to gossip about. This in turn
creates an interest amongst those who hear and in some
instances curiosity becomes such that they come to find out
for themselves. One Sunday evening I was approached by a
man with a pronounced European accent. He asked me if I
would pray for him to know Jesus. I replied that it would be
my privilege but suggested that we first talked. It transpired
that he was Dutch and six weeks previously had visited
London on a business trip. One of our fellowship had
entertained him and spoken about Jesus and what He was
doing in her life and that of our church. He was fascinated
and accepted an invitation to accompany her to a service and

see for himself. He told me that on arrival his first impression
was of a presence amongst the people. This he had interpreted
as relating in some way to God. Such was his growing interest
that for five weeks he commuted from Amsterdam on Sunday
afternoons in order to attend the evening service. During that
time he had come to realise that Jesus was the key to knowing
God and experiencing Him.

It is important to note that he was first conscious of the
presence of God when he came into a worshipping
congregation. The psalmist tells us that God is 'enthroned
upon the praises of Israel' (Psalm 22:3, Revised Standard
Version). Whereas Paul reminds the church at Corinth that
they are the temple of the Holy Spirit, implying that God is
in the midst of a Spirit-filled people. Besides the general
awareness of God which many people initially sense, there
are the manifestations of the Holy Spirit which are themselves
evangelistic. During our regular worship it is quite normal
for the congregation to sing in tongues. This can be very
beautiful as hundreds of different languages harmonise under
the leading and inspiration of the Holy Spirit. I have often
been asked by visitors to explain what is happening and how
people can sing together in such a way without first having
learnt the language. When replying I speak simply of the
meaning of Jesus' death, resurrection and ascension and
emphasise how the presence of the Holy Spirit, which they
have experienced, is a sign that Jesus is Lord and ruling in
heaven. Words of knowledge, prophecy and healing can have
the same impact and lead a visitor to ask similar questions.

Although people initially may experience God in such ways,
it is crucial that the cross is at the centre of a congregation's
worship and fellowship. For it is the message of the cross which
introduces people to Jesus. Confession of a sin is an integral
part of worship and this gathering of the worshipping people
around the cross in order to confess and receive forgiveness
in Jesus' name is in itself evangelistic. All preaching should
have as its backcloth the crucifixion of Christ. The function
of the preacher is to speak of God's relationship with man

and its implications for daily living. He needs to be constantly teaching that such a relationship restores all relationships, not only with others but with oneself. However, the greatest evangelistic act of worship is the Lord's Supper. Here in the symbols of bread and wine the death of Jesus for man's sin is portrayed in a most vivid and powerful way. During a meal on the night prior to His death it is recorded that, 'Jesus took bread, gave thanks and broke it, and gave it to his disciples, saying "Take and eat; this is my body." Then he took the cup, gave thanks and offered it to them, saying, "Drink from it, all of you. This is my blood of the covenant, which is poured out for many for the forgiveness of sins" ' (Matthew 26:26–28). I have known many people who have come to faith in Christ as the Holy Spirit has enlightened their minds to the real meaning of the bread and wine. I remember on one occasion giving the bread to a person with the words, 'This is the body of Christ. It is a sign of God's love for you expressed in Christ's death on the cross. Give thanks to God.' He told me later that it was as he started to thank God for Christ's death for him that faith was born in his heart.

Whenever the Church comes together to worship there always needs to be an opportunity for those who have been moved by the Holy Spirit to receive prayer. At St Andrew's we give such an invitation after all our services. The Dutchman I mentioned had, over a number of weeks, experienced a combination of all the ingredients I have described. These had all been signs which had led him to Jesus Christ. He had come to realise that a decision needed to be made, and an opportunity for this was provided.

Introducing people to Jesus within the confines of a building, and on a church's terms, should be the normal experience of every congregation in which the cross is being preached and the Holy Spirit honoured. This is what happened in the first Christian meetings in Jerusalem. Shortly after Pentecost, Luke recorded that '. . . the Lord added to their number daily those who were being saved' (Acts 2:47). The new converts were obviously being drawn by the life of the group of believers who themselves were particularly conscious of the presence and power of the risen Lord working in their midst.

As God visits the Church in powerful manifestations of His love, the challenge confronting us is to take the Good News of Jesus from the building into the community and on into the world. Since coming to know Christ myself I have always been intrigued by the way in which others find Him. In the many testimonies I have elicited there is one common thread. The majority of new converts initially experienced an act of kindness from a Christian. This kind act became a major signpost on their journey to faith in Jesus Christ. Kindness is one of the character changes which is brought about in a Christian by the working of the Holy Spirit. Today this quality is especially powerful because we live in a society which is becoming more and more preoccupied with self cult and the cult of selfishness. It is as we relate in kindness to our immediate neighbours and work colleagues that we shall find many opportunities to share the Gospel of Christ.

One autumn our eldest son and I spent a week's holiday together in Cornwall. We both enjoy outdoor pursuits and decided to walk the North Cliffs from St Ives to Land's End. As we left Cape Cornwall we came to a holiday cottage which nestled on the cliff top overlooking the bay. This belonged to a family I had come to know fourteen years previously as the result of leading a mission to their village church. We stopped outside the cottage and I described the family to Jonathan and reminisced on how I had come to know them.

After about an hour the path took us to a large sweep of beach called Sennen Cove. Clambering down the path, I noticed two elderly people sunbathing in the shelter of the rocks. The couple were David and Jean Trehair, the friends I had been describing to Jonathan. We were all surprised at the meeting. Sitting together, we caught up on the events surrounding our respective families. I noticed that David related easily to Jonathan and they seemed to enjoy each other's company. A week or so after returning home,

Jonathan received a letter from David which included a generous monetary gift. In the note he told Jonathan that since their meeting he had been constantly praying for him. This act of kindness simply overwhelmed Jonathan who had not been to church for six years and always felt that God did things for other people, but not for him. The monetary gift had met an urgent need.

God followed David's act of kindness in a most wonderful way. On returning home from a morning staff meeting, I called to Jonathan to join me for coffee, as it was his day off. He replied that he would join me in a few minutes, after finishing his bath. As he did not appear, I busied myself. After half an hour he came into the kitchen clothed in a towel and weeping. It transpired that as I called him he went to climb out of the bath, and was overwhelmed by a power he seemed unable to resist. As he lay in the bath waves of love flowed over him. Another time, while working at a local greengrocer's shop, he was standing by the potatoes when suddenly his mind was filled with the thought that in Jesus he had eternal life. This revelation was so vivid that he kept sharing it with us for many days. To him it was a source of great joy. Within a few months he was on a Discipleship Training School with Youth With a Mission.

As you read this account of the spontaneous expansion of the early Church you cannot but be excited at the ways in which the Good News of Jesus Christ was taken to cities throughout the Mediterranean basin and beyond. A closer examination will reveal that this happened as ordinary men and women were prompted and led by the Holy Spirit. After the martyrdom of Stephen there was a persecution and the Church was scattered. The leaders stayed in Jerusalem but the people travelled far and wide sharing the message of Jesus as they went. Much of this took place outside buildings, and in places where people naturally gathered. The disciples of Jesus were the model. Jesus did not send them out to prearranged gatherings, but rather to the 'market-places' of the towns and villages. Whenever I read of this basic form

of evangelism it always fills me both with excitement and a
sense of dread. In what ways, I wondered, could this approach
be used today? I was to discover an answer to this on a tour
of New Zealand with a Faith Sharing Team.

Christian Advance Ministries had invited us to minister at
ten centres in New Zealand. This involved travelling from
Dunedin in the far south to Auckland in the North Island.
When we arrived at the river city Wanganui, to lead a
weekend for the churches, we had a Saturday conference
culminating in an evangelistic meeting in the Memorial Hall.
On the Sunday our team went out in twos to minister in the
surrounding churches. I went to Christ Church where Don
Battley is the vicar. Their main morning service was a
Eucharist. Next to the spontaneous form of worship, I was
greatly encouraged by the predominance of young couples and
teenagers who were present. This was a church seemingly
bursting with life. After I had preached, I sat and prayed
quietly as people were receiving the bread and wine. Suddenly
I had a most vivid impression. I saw streets with people
walking along them. Some of those walking had a sense of
purpose whilst others were apparently just filling in the time.
As I watched, the streets became fields of wheat. This was
superimposed by an old-fashioned sickle which was placed in
my hands. As I received it I started to weep. The tears of
intense compassion were with me throughout the day. This
vision and experience had a special significance.

When it came to what is termed 'mass evangelism' the
model I had was the one used successfully in the fifties and
early sixties by evangelists such as Billy Graham. The method
was simple. The churches in a given area or city combined
and hired a large stadium for a week of meetings. The
evangelist's team arrived some weeks prior to the proposed
meetings in order to train both counsellors and a choir. This
method was certainly successful in those days and I owe my
conversion to Christ to such a crusade. However, this
approach has many difficulties today. The average person has
little or no Christian background. If they attend, they find

it difficult to relate to a situation where enthusiastic people are singing songs they have never heard and using terminology which is foreign to them. However, if they do find such a meeting helpful and wish to find out more about faith in Christ then their immediate problem could well be that churches in their area have ceased to have relevance to the present.

It is our experience that the majority of people who attend such meetings are either committed Christians or already halfway to faith and involved in some way with a local church. At a major London crusade we had thirty people referred to us as converts. After visiting them all we found one to be a convert and the other twenty-nine to be committed Christians who took the opportunity to rededicate their lives to Christ. There is certainly a need for this to happen, but a Christian Celebration meeting is much the better context.

At Wanganui we had such an evangelistic event. Don Battley, with leaders from the major denominations, organised a city-wide meeting. In preparation, prayer groups were formed and every home in the city was visited with a personal invitation. Large banners advertising the meeting hung across all the major roads. Newspapers carried large advertisements and posters were prominent in house and shop windows. I was interviewed at length on local radio and our team was given much media publicity. On Saturday evening the Memorial Hall was comfortably filled by eight hundred people. I preached a simple Gospel message and concluded with a prayer of commitment. I then invited those who had responded to witness to Christ by walking to the front. Only six people came forward.

Later, I invited the Holy Spirit to minister and He came in great power, anointing and healing many. However, the main object of the evening was to introduce seekers to Christ but it was obvious that the people were all committed Christians. On our way to the hall I had noticed that in the parks and surrounding shopping malls there were hundreds of people sitting in the evening sun, either talking or playing informal ball games. There were gangs of youths, both Maori

and white, courting couples, elderly people and young
children. Those we were wanting to reach with the love of
Christ were actually outside the building. On the way home
Don remarked to me that we should have met in the park
and shared the Good News on the streets.

For the rest of the tour I kept emphasising the fact that the
Holy Spirit was coming in power to equip the church to
witness, and this included the market-place. This message
again created frustration within me and the people to whom
I spoke. There was a missing key. The real question was,
'How do we share the Gospel outside the church or similar
building?'

The following year Christian Advance Ministries invited
me back with a team. The invitation was to minister at their
summer schools and to lead two conferences for leaders who
felt a calling to share the Gospel of Christ in the market-place.
I prepared for the summer schools but still could not see how
we could share Christ in a relevant way on the streets.

We arrived at the Apostolic Training Centre which nestles
in the hills above Paraparumi. The site commands an
exquisite view of the beach and Kapiti Island. The following
day delegates arrived from all parts of the islands; I noticed
from the attendance list that it was going to be thoroughly
ecumenical and included a large number of clergy and their
wives.

It was John's birthday. He and his young wife, Debbie,
had been with us the previous year and were keen to witness
on the streets. After the party celebrations we were talking
together when John asked me what we were doing for the
following four days. His question sent waves of panic through
me. I took my leave from the team and walked towards my
room. On the way I was met by a raw-boned deer farmer.
He greeted me with the customary 'G'dye', and enquired
when we were going to get on with it! I slunk into my
bedroom.

I read again the first few chapters of the Acts of the Apostles
and a familiar saying of Jesus seemed to jump out at me. It

was where He told His disciples that, when the Holy Spirit came, they would receive power and witness to Him. During the last ten years I had been in hundreds of situations where the Holy Spirit had come in power, but rarely had those involved taking Christ on to the streets.

As I pondered on these things, the meaning of 'witness' suddenly dawned on me. I remembered that in the original Greek it meant 'martyr'. A 'witness' was a person who laid down his life in order that people might hear the message of Christ. In many situations today Christians are called upon to do this literally. However, I saw it could have a much wider meaning. Witnessing was an aspect of taking up the cross. To witness in the market-place, a person had to die to what people thought, to be prepared, like Jesus, to be ridiculed, laughed at and abused. If we were prepared to 'die', then the Holy Spirit would come in power.

My thoughts went next to the way in which Jesus instructed the various groups of disciples before sending them out with the Good News. Firstly He equipped them with His authority and power. As a policeman has the authority to stop a speeding car, so too he has the power of the law to make that authority effective. In the same way, Jesus gave His disciples authority over demons and diseases as well as the power to expel the demons and heal the sick.

As I reflected, I noticed that He commissioned them not only to speak but to act. They were to spread the Good News of the Kingdom of God, and then heal the sick, raise the dead, cleanse those with skin diseases and drive out demons. After the commission He gave practical instructions. They were to travel in twos, not only to provide companionship and support, but so that the individuals they met would not be overwhelmed. Above all else they were to travel light and be completely dependent on God for any need that arose. I saw in a new light how simple Jesus had been. I decided that the following day we would take Jesus' teaching literally and actually say and do what He commanded. Needless to say, that night I slept rather fitfully!

The first day of the conference dawned bright as a hundred leaders converged. In the first session I asked if people would share their expectations for the three days. Everyone who spoke said the same – they wanted to share the Good News in the market-places where the community gathered. The majority knew what it meant to be filled with the Holy Spirit but had not been able to translate that experience into sharing their faith and winning converts for Jesus. The Holy Spirit's filling had given them a new love for and confidence in Jesus, but it had also created frustrations. They wanted to share Him, but they had no model for doing so.

After the talk-back I simply reminded the leaders of what Jesus taught and how He had commissioned His disciples. I emphasised the need to be prepared to embrace the cross and die to self in order that they might speak for Jesus. It was agreed that the following morning we would wait upon God and then go out as the Holy Spirit directed us.

At the meeting that evening I taught how we could minister in the power of the Holy Spirit. This is covered in depth in my colleague David Pytches' book, *Come Holy Spirit*. Basic to this teaching is the belief that the Holy Spirit will always come if He is invited in the name of Jesus, whether this prayer is made in a church, store, pub, shopping mall, train or park. That evening I asked for some words of knowledge and then had our team praying with those who responded. For all of us, the transferring of this ministry from the security of a believing group into the streets of an unknown town was an enormous leap. Before closing the meeting I invited the Holy Spirit to come and empower us for the task. We waited patiently for about twenty minutes before He came to touch many with His power and love.

Whilst reading the Acts of the Apostles I have always been intrigued by the way in which the apostles were led by the Holy Spirit. On one of Paul's travels, the Holy Spirit had kept him from preaching in Asia and then stopped him and his team going into Bithynia. This was in order that they might take the Gospel into Europe via Philippi. The Lord had communicated this part of the plan to them through a vision.

Before we went out into the market-places I wanted to know what the Lord's plan was for this occasion, so the following morning we all gathered to wait upon Him. During this time it seemed right to me that we witness along the Kapiti coast, from Tawa in the south to Levin in the north, taking in the towns of Otaki, Waikanae, Plimmerton and Porirua. We divided into groups and made our way to these six destinations. Here the teams divided into twos to go out and to say and do what Jesus had commanded.

I went to Levin with Shirley from our team. With great fear and trepidation we made our way to the local park where we thought people might have gathered. As we approached the gate a lady, who must have been in her seventies, came running out in great distress. She was shaking all over and hardly coherent. It transpired that she had been mugged by two young men. We were sympathetic and listened as she related what had happened a number of times. Shirley then asked if she would like us to pray. She indicated that she would, so we invited the Holy Spirit to come and release her from fear and the memory of her ordeal. He came gently and we could see Him resting upon her. Her turmoil was being replaced by that 'peace which passes all understanding'.

Whilst this was happening we were standing on a main thoroughfare and people began to stare, wondering what we were doing with our hands on the head of an elderly lady. I started to feel embarrassed and was all for moving on, but I knew we could not because the Holy Spirit was still resting on her. I thought of the cross and died a little death.

The elderly lady was so delighted with what the Lord had done for her that she went peacefully on her way. We then went on into the park. Sitting on a roundabout was a young Maori woman with two small children. We commented on how her children were so obviously enjoying themselves as they jumped on and off. Within a few minutes I sensed this as a 'God appointment'.

The woman said she had been to church in her early teens

and had not been back since. However, she often thought
about God and had recently been wondering whether there
was any way one could actually get to know Him. Shirley
shared the Gospel of Jesus with her and we answered a
number of searching questions. She indicated that she would
like us to pray with her to receive Christ. She stood, closed
her eyes and opened her hands. We invited the Holy Spirit
to come and reveal Jesus to her. People passing by were giving
us rather odd looks. Again I reminded myself that we were
doing what we believed Jesus had told us to do, and we needed
to forget all about ourselves and what people might be thinking
or saying.

The rest of the day progressed in a similar fashion and we
were longing to meet up with the rest of our team to hear
what had happened with them. At the team rendezvous
Shirley and I were initially unable to share, as everyone was
bubbling with excitement at what they had seen God doing.
Needless to say, we were all eagerly awaiting the evening
report-back when all the teams would share.

At the evening meeting it was difficult getting people quiet
so that we could all be heard. It reminded me of Jesus'
disciples returning to Him, which in fact we were.

It would seem that the early Christians in Jerusalem
established a regular outdoor site where they could meet and
witness. It was called Solomon's Colonnade and here the
crowd gathered after the healing of the crippled man by Peter
and John. However, besides witnessing in twos and groups
individual believers, led by the Holy Spirit, took every
opportunity that He gave to share Christ. For they knew that
the Holy Spirit's power was given not that they should have
nice feelings, but they should witness to Christ's liberating
power to the lost world.

When Jesus called His first disciples He said to the
fishermen, 'Come with me, and I will teach you to catch men'
(Matthew 4:19, Good News Bible). The operative word is
'teach', implying that catching men for Jesus requires as much
skill as the fishermen had acquired in their profession. The

skills for this new ministry would all be learnt as the disciples
were prepared to die to what people thought of them, in order
to speak about Jesus. Through teaching and example He sent
them out with the following caution:

> I am sending you out like sheep among wolves. Therefore
> be as shrewd as snakes and as innocent as doves. Be on
> your guard against men; they will hand you over to the
> local councils and flog you in their synagogues . . . Brother
> will betray brother to death, and a father his child; children
> will rebel against their parents and have them put to death.
> (Matthew 10:16–17, 21)

If it is true that God so loved the world that He gave Jesus
to it in order that whoever believes in Him should not perish
but have eternal life (John 3:16), then God must be always
and at all times seeking to make Jesus known. This means
that on any street, at any time, in any part of the world, there
are people whom the Holy Spirit wants to introduce to Jesus.
He can do this sovereignly, but His main appointed way is
through a believer.

There has been a great emphasis on receiving the power
of the Spirit in order that we may witness. For the power to
have an outlet we need to learn to listen to God so that in
the 'market-place' He can give us what I would term 'God
Appointments'. I have discovered that God chooses some
strange places to introduce Himself. One of my most
embarrassing moments happened outside the Indian Embassy
in London. To receive a visa for India, it is necessary to go
to an office and make an application and then return the
following day to collect it. The office where you receive the
visa opens out on to a square where people queue sometimes
fifty deep, depending on the time of year.

Whilst in the queue I started a conversation with a young
man behind me who was planning to travel by train to the
major cities in India over a period of six months. After we
had discussed this in some detail, I felt the Holy Spirit prompt

me to turn and talk to a young woman. As it transpired, she was a medical student. Again, it was a death before I could tell her, in the hearing of all, that I was a Christian and going to India to talk about Jesus. Her reply confirmed to me that it was the Lord prompting the meeting.

She told me her brother at Cambridge had just become what people call 'born again'. Whatever the experience was, it had made him a much more loving and concerned brother. Since his experience she had wanted to meet someone who could answer her questions about being 'born again'. The queue was going extremely slowly and I was able to answer many of her thoughtful questions. I asked her if she wanted to receive Christ, and she replied that she did. This was an even bigger death! To this day, I wonder what people in the queue thought as I laid hands upon her and prayed.

The way ahead will not be found in the large evangelistic meeting to which a number of people will come to hear an internationally famous evangelist, nor in groups witnessing together on the streets, but rather as we accept the implications of discipleship, at the heart of which is death to self in order to speak for God. This involves us learning to know the voice of God in order that we may obey the promptings of His Spirit, wherever and whenever this may occur. For this spontaneous form of evangelism to take place, it must flow from a Church that is spiritually alive and relevant. It becomes 'another way'.

Chapter 12

DISCIPLES OF JESUS

One of the first books I ever read on Christian discipleship was by a German martyr, Dietrich Bonhoeffer. He aptly summarised the subject in the words, 'When Christ calls a man, he calls him to come and die'. Bonhoeffer was reflecting on the call of Jesus:

> If anyone would come after me, he must deny himself and take up his cross and follow me. For whoever wants to save his life will lose it, but whoever loses his life for me and for the gospel will save it. (Mark 8:34)

This truth is pursued powerfully by Paul when he speaks of being crucified with Christ, and that he no longer lived but Christ lived in him. The dying to self implies the reception of a new life.

One of the most awe-inspiring moments in my life was to be present at the birth of our daughter Noonie. In a conversation with a Jewish leader and theologian, Jesus uses this analogy of human birth to illustrate what He means by spiritual birth. He states that the only way into this world is through physical birth and implies that the only way to 'see' or 'enter' the Kingdom of God is through spiritual birth (John 3:1ff).

The mystery of life starts at conception and for a further nine months the embryo grows in secret, hidden within its mother's womb. Spiritual conception can happen in a variety

of ways. It often starts when a person first relates the creation
to an origin outside of themselves. This can come in a
moment of inspiration. A person may be watching a familiar
sunset or sunrise, or pauses on a clear night to stare into
the star studded universe, or holds a delicate multi-coloured
flower in his hand when, for a split second, he is made aware
of the possibility of God being the creator.

This initial seed implanted by the Holy Spirit starts to
grow and mature within the heart. Some people may start
to ask God for help and find their requests being answered.
Others may have, over many years, a series of what seem
to be chance meetings. On such occasions they meet
Christians who talk with them about Jesus Christ and the
meaning of His life. Maybe they are given experience based
Christian books, or accept an invitation to a Christian
meeting. There are numerous ways in which God speaks
to the heart and as this is taking place a hunger to know
God grows. This work of the Spirit gives birth to a spiritual
life, the moment the seeker receives Jesus. John in his Gospel
writes, 'Yet to all who received him, to those who believed
in his name, he gave the right [power] to become children
of God – children born not of natural descent, nor of human
decision or a husband's will, but born of God' (John
1:12–13).

Spiritual birth can take a wide variety of forms. In India,
for example, it would seem from talking with Christians that
it is often as the result of a vision, dream or supernatural
revelation. When I first heard of such stories, they greatly
perplexed me. During my earlier trips to India I was taken
by my host to visit the estate of a Hindu who had recently
become a Christian. On arrival I received the customary
welcome, and after meeting the family, sat outside in the
late evening to hear the new disciple's story. He was suffering
from heart disease and had already experienced a number
of heart attacks. When lying in bed recovering from one,
he called upon God to help him. In response he saw standing
by his bed a figure of a man surrounded by light and full

of the most incredible love. He recognised the person as Jesus. Subsequently he called his Christian neighbour who explained to him more fully the way of Christ.

At the conference for the diocese of West Bengal which we led, a Hindu family related the following story. They had sent their daughter of eight to a school staffed by Christians. It was here that she first heard of Jesus Christ. Returning home one day, she stood looking in a mirror when she saw the figure of a man behind her. As she turned, the man showed her his hands; they had scars in the palms. He invited her to touch them. She recognised him as Jesus. She ran and told her mother of the experience. Her mother was sceptical whereas her father exploded in anger. He took a cane and beat her, furious that the Christians should brainwash his daughter. The girl was taken from the school and forbidden to speak of Jesus again. She was distraught and yet would not deny Jesus even though her father still continued to chastise her. Wonderfully for this little girl, the Lord intervened. Her father had a similar experience of the risen Christ. He was converted from Hinduism and, with his family, presented himself to the village pastor for baptism. The pastor took them all to Barrackpore so that they could relate the events to his Bishop, who welcomed them into the Christian family.

Here in the West spiritual birth is more likely to be either as the result of a prayer in private, or through that of a friend or pastor who acts as a spiritual midwife. However, there is one certain characteristic about birth: those who experience it know that they are living a life in a new dimension.

After our daughter was born the midwife wrapped her in a little sheet before handing her to me. I then laid her in Mary's arms. As a baby she was totally dependent upon her mother for nourishment. This initially took the form of milk but, before too long, solids were introduced and within a year she was doing her best to feed herself. The first year saw incredible growth but it involved a high degree of love, care, understanding and commitment from us as parents. A new disciple of Jesus Christ is, in spiritual terms, no different from our baby daughter. They need loving, caring, feeding and protecting by the fellowship of the Church. However, the goal of all nurturing is that the child learns to feed and take an ever-increasing degree of responsibility for itself.

A child slowly learns to know its parents and explore the new environment that it finds itself in. This is entirely different from the confines of the womb where nothing of its new world could ever have been conceived. For the new disciple, learning to know God is first and foremost through talking with Him. This always seems slightly strange to start with because God is not tangible. He cannot be known through the senses of touch, taste, sight or sound. He is Spirit and can only be known by those, who like the new disciple, have been made spiritually aware by God Himself. Often this communication is non-verbal. We live in a society which works together to suppress thoughts about the ultimate reality in human existence, which is the experience of death. This is brought into sharp focus when a notable personage dies. The deceased life is like a tiny pebble which has been dropped into a pond. Ripples run out from its entrance but within a short time the pond is still again and the pebble forgotten. Because modern man does not want to face up to the fact of his own death he fills his life to overflowing with activity and noise. One of the first areas that the new disciple needs to learn to enter is that of silence.

The Lord instructs David in the Psalms, 'Be still, and know that I am God' (Psalm 46:10). To be still literally means 'to let go'. This involves all situations which cause nagging anxieties and fears. Such situations need to be shared in detail with the Lord and then left with Him. We do this in response to the scriptural admonition where we are encouraged to, 'Cast all your anxiety on him because he cares for you' (1 Peter 5:7). The disciple can enter into the stillness because in Christ he has nothing to fear from silence, self or God. His meeting with God in the silence is an indication that the eternal world is already breaking into the present. He is experiencing a fellowship with One who is outside of time and space. This fellowship is spiritual and, because the spirit of the disciple continues after physical death, so will his relationship with and knowledge of God.

I find that if I am meeting new people I am inclined to be slightly nervous, and feel obliged to talk whenever the conversation lags. However, I find that the closer the friend, the less I feel I need to speak. The knowing of God in the silence is a similar experience. There are occasions when the communication is just being in His presence and knowing His love and peace. On other occasions God communicates with us simply and yet profoundly through the created order. In Psalm 19 David describes the silent sermon which is being spoken continually. 'The heavens declare the glory of God; the skies proclaim the work of his hands. Day after day they pour forth speech; night after night they display knowledge. There is no speech or language where their voice is not heard. Their voice goes out into all the earth, and their words to the ends of the world' (v. 1–4). By faith the new disciple understands that it was through God's word that the creation came into existence. In the world around him he perceives God's incredible creative power and hears Him speak.

We live near an extremely beautiful area of common land and, over two decades, I have walked its pathways and seen it in the scorching heat of summer, as well as the bitterness of winter when snow blocks its paths and torrents of rain turn it into a quagmire. Often, as I walk, I seek to create an inner stillness and to be aware of the Spirit of God speaking to me. Sometimes a picture in the creation is highlighted and becomes a parable in which I hear God speak. Jesus heard His Father in this way and encouraged others to do likewise. He pointed to the ploughed field and drew attention to the various areas which were having seed scattered on them. He taught that the ways in which the soil received the seeds depicted the ways in which men responded to His message (Mark 4:1ff).

I remember walking through the barren woods at the end of a particularly severe winter. My attention was drawn to tiny shoots of green which were appearing on the branches and starting to force their way out of the buds which imprisoned them so tightly. Standing still, I stared around me at this miracle of nature. Suddenly there came flooding into my mind the many churches which we had visited. Their common denominator was the experience of new expressions of spiritual life. The Holy Spirit seemed to be saying to me that it was springtime in the Church. On longer reflection, the parable within the creation was an apt picture of what has continued to happen.

God speaks in and through His creation yet it is supremely in His written word, the Bible, that God speaks to us. As a new disciple this can present a problem. Many people today were taught a religion at school which denied the authenticity of many of the incidents recorded in the Bible. There is a common consensus that scientific discoveries have proved the Scriptures to be largely inaccurate. The religion taught also involves a comparative study of Christianity with other major religions such as Islam which claims that God dictated the Koran to Mohammed, making it the very word of God. Against this background the dilemma facing the new disciple is what to believe in the Bible and what to discard as being inaccurate or just cultural.

Some years ago I was with a friend in New Zealand sailing around the islands at the southern end of the Hauraki Gulf. Before we left our moorings and sailed out of the Tamaki River we looked at a detailed chart of the area. This clearly showed the safest course, avoiding the dangerous rocks which lay submerged a few feet below the sea. The only way we could know that the chart was accurate and its information trustworthy was to use it. My friend, who owns a yacht hire company, had over many years proved to himself beyond any doubt that the charts could be trusted in all and every circumstance. At the end of the day in question I had also proved that on that particular journey they were reliable and trustworthy. It is the same way that a disciple of Jesus learns to prove for himself the trustworthiness of the Bible in life's many and varied circumstances.

At the end of my theological training I had many doubts about the reliability of the Scriptures. My tutors had quoted eminent theologians who maintained that some sayings and instances concerning Jesus were original whilst others were of unreliable authenticity. Such scholars divided up the Old Testament books in such a way that left one with the feeling that if God was in any way involved in the inspiration of the Scriptures it must have been on a limited basis. This left me confused and perplexed. In my frustration I took my Bible, knelt down, and told the Lord that by faith I accepted the Scriptures as authentic and authoritative for my understanding of Him and the way He intended me to live my life. This proved to be a watershed. My understanding changed and, looking back over many years, the biblical chart has always proved to be accurate. However, there are still sections I do not understand but trust that, as in the past, God will continue to reveal His truth to me.

Paul wrote a letter to one of his young disciples and referred to the Scriptures in this way. 'All Scripture is God-breathed and is useful for teaching, rebuking, correcting and training in righteousness, so that the man of God may be thoroughly equipped for every good work' (2 Timothy 3:16–17). I know new disciples of Jesus who started reading the Bible but stopped within a few weeks because they did not understand its message. With great enthusiasm we all started with the book of Genesis and became thoroughly lost somewhere between Adam and Noah. After re-reading the same chapters on a number of occasions, we ceased because it seemed so incomprehensible and apparently unrelating to our ordinary lives. The book of Genesis is obviously the wrong place to start. A New Testament Gospel such as Mark would give a better introduction. The opening sentence of this book states its theme: 'The beginning of the gospel about

Jesus Christ, the Son of God' (Mark 1:1). It is important that the new disciple sets about discovering for himself the content of the Good News. It is helpful to have a notebook nearby so that important discoveries can be jotted down and referred to at a later time. Probably the best place to start the Old Testament is with the Psalms. These have been the prayer book of the Christian Church from its beginning. Here with the psalmist we learn how to relate to God in all life's varied experiences and to turn the psalmist's prayers into ours. Next to the Psalms is the book of Proverbs which teaches us how to behave towards our fellow men. It is helpful to read these books in conjunction with one another.

The disciple's aim is to know the word of God. To help me to do this I regularly have a new Bible. I systematically read it through underlining important promises and scribbling in the margin my thoughts on what I have read. It is also important to commit promises and particularly helpful passages to memory. One summer, as a theological student, I worked at a girls' public school as the third gardener. I had responsibility for mowing the lawns. This was similar to painting the Forth Bridge – once the task was completed it was usually time to start again. Each morning I would write Scripture promises on cards and Sellotape them on the mower in front of me. As I traversed the lawns I committed these to memory. I have sought to continue this habit without the mower, and find that God often speaks words of encouragement to me by bringing to my remembrance His words which I have committed to memory. Maybe this is what David meant when he wrote, 'I have hidden your word in my heart that I might not sin against you' (Psalm 119:11).

Through the Scriptures God the Holy Spirit speaks generally and particularly. The Bible is a book about God so that, whatever we read, we are learning something about the nature of God and the ways in which He relates in love to man. However, there are occasions when a particular Scripture is illuminated by the Holy Spirit and seems to jump off the page. This is God speaking in a special way. When this occurs it is important that we meditate upon the meaning of the verse or verses. The psalmist writes of a disciple: 'But his delight is in the law of the Lord, and on his law he meditates day and night' (Psalm 1:2). The word in this context means 'to mutter', to speak in a low, barely audible voice. On the occasions when I experience this, I usually talk to myself about the verse, asking it questions, considering its meaning from a number of different angles. Finally I ask myself what practical steps I need to take to implement in my life what the Scripture has taught. The second meaning of the word meditate is 'to bow down' as in 'I meditate on your precepts and consider your ways' (Psalm 119:15). The act of bowing is that of paying homage. It implies that the disciple has heard God speak and is seeking to obey what he has heard. As James reminds his readers:

> Do not merely listen to the word, and so deceive yourselves. Do what it says. Anyone who listens to the word but does not do what it says is like a man who looks at his face in a mirror and, after looking at himself, goes away and immediately forgets what he looks like. But the man who looks intently into the perfect law that gives freedom and continues to do this, not forgetting what he has heard, but doing it – he will be blessed in what he does. (James 1:22–25)

Jesus said to any person contemplating becoming His disciple, 'If anyone would come after me, he must deny himself and take up his cross and follow me' (Mark 8:34). All that 'denying self' and 'taking up the cross' involves is revealed in the Scriptures. This 'doing' of the word of God is the basis of discipleship and a follower is soon confronted by the challenge of the cost.

Our society is particularly materialistic. Our highest priority is the acquisition of money and the commodities

which it may purchase. We judge people's success in life
in terms of their salary, house, model of car, consumer goods
and the area in which they live. The billions of pounds spent
each year on consumer advertising encourage us to be just
ahead of our neighbours by discarding the old model and
buying the new. This is one of the reasons we find it
particularly difficult to give away our highest prized
possession – money. The new disciple of Jesus will find
this to be an area that the Holy Spirit will soon start to
challenge him in. It is humorously stated that there are three
stages in true conversion. For some people it begins in the
mind, when they receive and believe the true facts about
Jesus Christ. Hopefully, this is followed by an eighteen-inch
drop when their belief enters the heart where the emotions
and feelings are. The third stage is often considered the
hardest, when conversion reaches the pocket where the
cheque book is.

At the start of our ministry Mary and I decided that we
would not mention any financial needs we might have
publicly but rather pray about them together. What I am
writing now is an exception and is simply to illustrate the
problem I faced when the Lord started to convert my pocket.
In 1967 we went to Cornwall to start our ministry. Our
annual salary was £650. We had a Mini, which we had been
given, and we were expected to use this to visit the homes
of many outlying parishioners as well as the sick in the
hospitals. The church we served did not pay any working
expenses in those days. After three years as students we had
£50 in the bank, which had not only to finance our move,
but also to furnish our new home. However, we did have
a great trust in God to supply our needs – that is, until
I started to feel uncomfortable about our giving.

In the reading of the Old Testament Scriptures, my
attention was regularly being drawn to the way the believers
tithed one tenth of their income to God. Up until then my
giving had been spasmodic and usually involved what I had
in my pocket. Now I sensed that the Lord was calling me

to give one tenth of our income. I kept dismissing this notion
as being absolutely impossible. Financially, we were just
managing to make ends meet, but Mary only owned two
dresses, our second child was imminent and the car was
needing a new gear box. To give away £65 a year seemed
irresponsible when we needed so much. I put the thought
to the back of my mind, thinking that in the future, when
my income increased, I would seriously reconsider the
possibility. However, the Lord continued to persist with me.

I was reading Luke's Gospel and came to the saying of
Jesus where He promised, 'Give, and it will be given to
you. A good measure, pressed down, shaken together and
running over, will be poured into your lap. For with the
measure you use, it will be measured to you' (Luke 6:38).
These words seemed to jump right off the page. They
confronted me with my meanness and unwillingness to be
obedient to God's voice. Again I reasoned with myself,
'Surely God couldn't be interested in my paltry £65!' In
my daily readings the psalmist had reminded me on many
occasions that 'the cattle on a thousand hills' belong to the
Lord. It was dawning on me that there were much deeper
implications in this call to tithe. As I struggled with the idea,
I started to understand that Jesus wanted me to acknowledge
that everything I had came from Him. One of the ways in
which I could express gratitude was by giving back to Him
a portion of what He had given me. Yet this needed to be
done with the right attitude – not grudgingly but in a spirit
of thankfulness and joy.

There was also another vital area. We could hardly
manage on what we had yet I realised that if we tithed it
would make us more dependent upon the Lord. Still, with
a certain degree of apprehension, I took a covenant form
from the church treasurer and committed us to tithe one
tenth of our salary. This decision put my relationship with
Jesus on a new footing. I started to trust Him for situations
in which I did not have the resources. Initially there was
the car's gear box and this was followed by the Mini sub-

frame. Inadvertently I had driven over a humpback bridge on Dartmoor at such a speed that the five of us were airborne for a few seconds. On landing, the car seemed to split in two. I recorded this expenditure in my diary and wondered how it was going to be met. I was to find that this giving of the tithe released money from the most unlikely sources. After a series of hospital visits, a grateful parishioner gave me a tankful of petrol. My mechanic, a dry old Cornishman, repaired my car with pieces from crashed vehicles and prided himself on keeping my bill to the minimum. I saw all this to be the hand of God for He said that if we seek His Kingdom in our lives, then He would add the things we need.

It is often in the area of money that the first major challenge to discipleship starts. As the follower goes on worshipping and listening to God, other areas are brought into focus so that more and more the discipline brings his life under the Lordship of Jesus. The ultimate outworking of this is to be found in a story which Jesus tells His disciples (Luke 17:7). At first what He describes appears to be grossly unfair. It concerns a ploughman who has worked the fields from the rising of the sun to its setting. Tired and physically exhausted, he returns to his employer. Having reminded the disciples of this common rural scene He asks them two questions. The first revolves around the way in which the servant would be received by his employer. Would he say to the returning ploughman, 'Come along now and sit down to eat' or 'Prepare my supper, get yourself ready and wait on me while I eat and drink; after that you may eat and drink?' The second question concerns the employer's attitude to his workman. 'Would he thank the servant because he did what he was told to do?' (v. 9).

The implication of this story is that the owner of the farm would receive his servant with a command to prepare supper and wait upon table. There would be no word of gratitude because the servant was only doing his duty. Jesus then applies this teaching to His disciples. 'So you also, when you have done everything you were told to do, should say "We are unworthy servants; we have only done our duty" ' (v. 10). He sees the disciples as being in the same role as the 'ploughman' in the story – they are His servants. We are not dealing here with a hired employee with union backed rights, but rather with a servant who was not of the British 'Upstairs, Downstairs' variety. The word Jesus uses for servant is 'doulos' which means a slave.

To start to understand the radical nature of this teaching, it is important to consider the culture in which the story was set. For a thousand years the economic and social life of the ancient Near East was based on slavery. Slaves could be the spoils of war, or the result of bankruptcy where the debtor and his family became part of the payment of the debt. In times of famine a man might voluntarily sell himself and family into slavery. The slave became the property of his owner and could be sold, leased or exchanged. He or she had neither rights nor wages, and could be beaten or abused at the will of the owner. Unique to Israel was the rule that after six years the slave was freed. However, if he wanted to remain with his owner then his ear was pierced and tagged as a sign that he was a slave for the rest of his life. Even when this happened his status remained unchanged. He was still the property of his owner. Bearing this in mind we can begin to understand the radical call of Jesus. The disciple was a 'slave to God' (Romans 6:22) and Jesus was the 'slave owner' (Ephesians 6:6).

Such a teaching is contrary to everything we know and value in our society today. Many of us are members of the state Church which gives the impression of being an institution of privilege, position and power. The largest percentage of church members belong to a suburban culture which applauds ambition, success and attainment, and is slightly critical of those who do not make the grade. Most are well educated and in leadership positions which are understood in terms of authority and power over others. It was no different in Jesus' day. In a conversation with James and John (Mark 10:35), He told them that although the leaders of their society were characterised by their power and authority over others, it was not to be so with them. 'Instead whoever wants to become great among you must be your servant, and whoever wants to be first must be slave of all. For even the Son of Man did not come to be served, but to serve, and to give his life as a ransom for many' (v. 43–45). We are disciples of Jesus Christ, who chose to become a man and take the nature of a slave. It was in this capacity that He lived and ministered for three years, serving the needs of men and women. It is to this office that He calls His disciples, that they might offer to the world 'another way'.

David Pytches

SOME SAID IT THUNDERED

David Pytches tells of his encounters with a few godly
men who believe that they have frequent revelations
directly from God, often accompanied by remarkable
signs, which they have then shared with their local
churches.

The author discusses how some prophecies have been
given and fulfilled, some are yet to be fulfilled, though
the accompanying sign has already appeared, and finally
why in other cases neither sign nor prophecy have been
fulfilled. The book concludes with suggestions on how
local church leadership can cope with and encourage the
potential prophet.

BISHOP DAVID PYTCHES was Bishop of the Diocese of
Chile, Bolivia and Peru and is now the Vicar of St
Andrew's, Chorleywood. He is the author of COME,
HOLY SPIRIT and DOES GOD SPEAK TODAY?

David Pytches

DOES GOD SPEAK TODAY?

David Pytches asserts that God speaks to people today, in their everyday situations, and provides many instances where God can be said to have been at work.

This book contains a selection of true stories, many from his and his wife's pastoral and personal experience, some from other countries. They show how people have been led into all kinds of blessings, big and small, by responding to what they believed to be a revelation from God. David Pytches also details many instances where people have been convinced they heard the voice of God — only to be proved wrong, thus adding validity to what could otherwise be a one-sided account. He finishes with balanced biblical teaching on guidance and the need for discernment.

Mary Pytches

YESTERDAY'S CHILD

'This is a book for all who would be healed, or be used in prayer for the healing of others.'
From the foreword by *Leanne Payne*

Mary Pytches' counselling experience has firmly convinced her that we are today the result of our past. In YESTERDAY'S CHILD she lifts the veil of our foundational years of childhood, where situations and experiences, often forgotten, influence us as adults. She takes the reader on a stage-by-stage description of the growing process, breaking development into the stages of 0–12 months, 15 months–3 years, 3–6 years, 6–12 years and finally adolescence. Each chapter ends with practical questions and exercises in self-analysis, helping the reader to come to terms with his/her own past to allow positive healing.

Mary Pytches, wife of Bishop David Pytches, has helped develop pastoral counselling at St Andrew's, Chorleywood. She is author of SET MY PEOPLE FREE and A HEALING FELLOWSHIP.

Tom Smail

THE FORGOTTEN FATHER

The charismatic movement, with its emphasis on the
Holy Spirit, has grown in recent years. Tom Smail
contends that the Christian Gospel is essentially a Father
movement. He believes that the first priority for Christian
life is to rediscover the Father. He examines Jesus'
relationship with his Father, and then clarifies how our
relationship to God the Father can come alive, showing
what it means to be able to say through the Spirit 'Abba,
Father'.

THOMAS SMAIL was Director of the Fountain Trust and
Vice-Principal of St John's Theological College,
Nottingham. He is now a trustee of the C S Lewis Centre
and Rector of All Saints' Church, Sanderstead.